Praise for

"*Effortless Savings* is a practical manual on frugality and building savings. Richard's ideas are easy to read and even easier to apply. His end of chapter action points give readers an understandable road map to reaching their financial goals. This book isn't about complex formulas and calculations; it's about evaluating your time and using it to maximize your savings."

Steve & Annette Economides
New York Times **best-selling authors**
America's Cheapest Family Gets You Right on the Money

"*Effortless Savings* is also effortless reading, a light and breezy guidebook that can yield weighty results. Richard Syrop's tips often go beyond the usual which led me to highlighting ideas on nearly every page. Short but sweet, "*Effortless Savings*" will galvanize you to make numerous and painless spending cuts and live more abundantly."

Lorilee Craker
New York Times **best-selling author**
Money Secrets of the Amish

"*Effortless Savings* is full of tips that everyday people with regular expenses can begin using right away. This book is not for the black belt frugalistas who can squeeze each penny until it screams for mercy, choosing to live without internet or cell phones....this book is for the person with regular family-style expenses who wants to cut their telecom bills in half."

Deborah Taylor-Hough
Author of *Frugal Living for Dummies*®
TheSimpleMom.com

"Chock full of money-saving ideas, *Effortless Savings* pays for itself before you finish the first chapter. A great guide for any cost-conscious consumer. Syrop's meticulously researched book makes saving easy."

Jon Yates
Author of *What's Your Problem?*

Praise for *Effortless Savings*

"*Effortless Savings* is full of practical strategies that can help anyone save big money on everyday expenses. Richard Syrop offers solid advice and a fresh voice on the simple truth that taking control of your spending is the best way to give yourself a raise."

Mary Hunt
Founder of Debt-Proof Living and best-selling author
The Smart Woman's Guide to Planning for Retirement

"Richard Syrop's book is absolutely the real thing! It's practical, simple, easy to read, and it definitely delivers. Open this book to any page and the advice given will be sound, easily-applied and effortlessly life-changing. Buy this book, and then get out your yellow marker!"

JoAnneh Nagler
Author of *The Debt-Free Spending Plan*

"*Effortless Savings* is the economic Swiss Army knife you've been looking for. This easy to read savings manifesto will help you reclaim the power in your relationships with service providers, painlessly change your habits, and put a few more bills back in your wallet. An authentic life-hackers guide to the savings universe."

Christopher Greenslate
Co-author of *On a Dollar a Day*

"*Effortless Savings* is loaded with practical tips for saving money on all of your daily expenses. If you diligently follow Syrop's suggestions, you *will* save money."

J.D. Roth
Founder of the award-winning website GetRichSlowly.org

Praise for *Effortless Savings*

"What an informative book! As a personal finance author, I pride myself in saving money and being as frugal as possible. "*Effortless Savings*" helps me take being able to save money up a few notches. Richard shows us how to save on almost anything we can think of – from car insurance to airline tickets to even the clothes we wear. This book is a must-read for anyone looking to get the most out of their money."

Danny Kofke
Author of *A Simple Book of Financial Wisdom*

"Whether you're trying to get out of debt or save for the future, every dollar counts. In *Effortless Savings*, Richard Syrop helps you find those dollars which can add up to big savings."

Gerri Detweiler
Author and host of Talk Credit Radio
The Ultimate Credit Handbook

"*Effortless Savings* is a great one-stop shop resource for anyone serious about stretching their money."

Carrie Rocha
Author of *Pocket Your Dollars*
PocketYourDollars.com

"Without forcing the reader to become obsessive over savings, Richard provides an easy-to-follow formula for reducing expenses in dozens of areas of everyday life. You won't have to follow every suggestion, but by choosing just a few, you will be on your way to effortlessly saving. Before you know it, your days of paycheck-to-paycheck living will be behind you."

Michael B. Rubin
Author of *Beyond Paycheck to Paycheck*

Praise for *Effortless Savings*

"Effortless indeed; don't miss this gem! Chock full of insider information Richard provides practical tips that work for your life. Seriously I know lots of ways to save money but this book even had me saying "Why didn't I think of that?" Like me, you'll find yourself flagging ideas on almost every page. Purchase this book today and start saving money tomorrow!"

Jamie Novak
Author of *Stop Throwing Money Away*

"As a naturally frugal person, I've been collecting money-saving ideas for years. But a couple hours with Richard Syrop's book "*Effortless Savings*" gave me at least a dozen more doable ways to save, in areas ranging from auto insurance to home heating to eye care to travel and entertainment. Implementing even a couple ideas in this book will quickly recoup the cost of the book, but my guess is that most readers will find many new tricks to keep hard-earned bucks in their pockets."

Mary Ostyn
Author of *Family Feasts for $75 a Week*
Owlhaven.net

"*Effortless Savings* offers a great checklist of money saving tips for anyone who wants to cut some fat from their budget."
David Ning
Founder of MoneyNing.com

"Unless you're a monk, you've probably never been excited by the idea of sacrifice. We want to save money and be kind to the planet, but only if it's not too hard and doesn't require us to give up the experiences that make life fun. Full of clever yet commonsense tips, *Effortless Savings* is a comprehensive guide to accessing the things we love, without wasting time or money."

Beth Buczynski
Author of *Sharing Is Good*

EFFORTLESS SAVINGS

A MONEY MANAGEMENT GUIDE
TO SAVING WITHOUT SACRIFICE

RICHARD SYROP

Published by:
White Willow Press
Post Office Box 45293
Seattle, WA 98145
www.whitewillowpress.com

ISBN# 9780989015608
e-ISBN# 9780989015615
LCCN# 2013943784

Publisher's Cataloging-in-Publication
(Provided by Quality Books, Inc.)
Syrop, Richard.
    Effortless savings : a money management guide to
saving without sacrifice / Richard Syrop.
    pages cm
    Includes index.
    LCCN 2013943784
    ISBN 9780989015608
    ISBN 9780989015615

    1. Finance, Personal. 2. Saving and investment.
I. Title.

HG179.S97 2013   332.024
                        QBI13-600127

CONTENTS

CHAPTER EIGHT
ADDITIONAL SHOPPING STRATEGIES

CHAPTER NINE
RESTAURANTS AND ENTERTAINMENT

CHAPTER TEN
VACATIONS AND TRAVEL EXPENSES

CHAPTER ELEVEN

CREDIT CARDS AND BANKING

INTRODUCTION

A NEW APPROACH TO SAVINGS

The goal of *Effortless Savings* is to help you save money, lots of money, without sacrificing any of the things you enjoy. Although accomplishing this may sound unrealistic, it's actually quite easy. In the following chapters, presented in a simple, step-by-step format, you will discover hundreds of painless, practical strategies that can save you thousands of dollars a year. If you implement just a few of them, not only will you reduce your expenses but you will probably find yourself buying and doing several things you previously thought you couldn't afford.

Throughout this book, I have attempted to cover all of the major expenses affecting American consumers, including telecom, insurance and home energy bills, as well as groceries, toiletries, clothing, automobile upkeep, entertainment, dining out, and travel costs. I have categorized these expenses (and many others) into clearly defined chapters, which are more or less independent of each other. As a result, you can read them in whatever order you like.

Rest assured, no matter which chapter you're reading, you won't find penny-pinching ideas designed to save just a few cents here and there. Instead, you will find saving methods that target the major offenders of wasteful spending. Of course, not all of these suggestions will be relevant to your lifestyle, but most of them will be, regardless of your income.

So what are you waiting for? Let's get started.

CHAPTER ONE

TELECOM SERVICES

Thanks to the thriving competition in the telecommunications industry, it's quite easy to find voice, video, and Internet service for great rates. The following suggestions should help you maintain or improve the services you have now, while giving your bills a much-needed haircut.

CELL PHONES

Pay Reasonable Rates Without a Contract

Major wireless carriers love nothing more than to rope consumers into twenty-four-month contracts. For years they have successfully lured us into these deals with flashy free phones and other gimmicks. Although signing up for a long-term deal may not sound so bad on the surface, it takes away all your power as a consumer and forces you to pass up new and better offers as they emerge. Could you ever imagine giving a grocery, drug, or department store a long-term business commitment? Assuming your answer is no, why should you look at cell phone service any differently?

Thankfully, there are a handful of service providers that use the same networks as major carriers but have much cheaper rates and do not require a contract. These companies are referred to as mobile virtual network operators (MVNOs). MVNOs typically purchase wholesale service in bulk from Verizon, AT&T, T-Mobile, or Sprint. They then set their own pricing and market it under their own brands.

Most MVNOs will not require you to buy a cell phone from them as a condition of getting wireless service. Instead, they will generally let you use any device you want, as long as it is compatible with whatever network a particular MVNO is using. This provides a great opportunity to switch carriers without being forced to make an unnecessary investment.

Some of the better MVNOs to consider include Page Plus Cellular (Verizon's network), Straight Talk (AT&T's network), PlatinumTel (T-Mobile's network), and Boost Mobile (Sprint's network). Plans from all these companies are around 40 percent less than similar deals from major telecom carriers.

The main drawback to getting service from an MVNO is that most of these companies tend to employ a skeleton staff to keep their rates as low as possible. As a result, when you call an MVNO's help line, you should expect to be put on hold longer than usual. In addition, MVNOs that use Verizon's network do not presently have access to their 4G LTE services. However, this is likely to change in the future.

Consider Prepaid Plans

Prepaid plans are a good option if you use fewer than five hundred minutes per month, don't send many text messages, and aren't big on mobile Internet use. Although most major carriers have prepaid plans, MVNOs offer nearly identical services for half the cost. For the past few years, Page Plus Cellular and PlatinumTel have had the most reasonable prepaid rates on reliable networks. Page Plus tends to be the better choice if you make a lot of phone calls, whereas PlatinumTel is a great option if you send a lot of text messages and occasionally want to get on the Internet.

When considering prepaid service, keep in mind that you will not receive a monthly bill and will never have to deal with unexpected fees and taxes. Additionally, because prepaid plans do not require a contract, you don't have to worry about early termination fees if you want to switch carriers down the line. Despite prepaid plans being an ideal choice for many consumers, most wireless companies rarely recommend this option. The reason for this is they make very little money off of this service. After all, you only pay for the minutes you use, as opposed to buying extra time that goes down the drain or is put into a rollover account that collects dust.

Get Out of Your Contract

If you would like to get wireless service from an MVNO but are currently locked into a contract, you may be able to get out of it without paying early termination fees. Every major cell phone carrier will allow you to transfer your contract to another person, whether you have two months or two years left on your commitment. While this may sound like a hopeless task, transferring a contract is actually fairly easy, thanks to a few innovative websites.

CellSwapper.com and CellTradeUSA.com are the two leading matchmakers for wireless contracts. To put your contract on the market with either of them, all you have to do is create a free account and listing. Although both sites charge around twenty dollars for their service, you will not be billed until your contract is taken over.

On top of saving someone activation fees, it's also advisable to offer either your cell phone or twenty to thirty dollars as an additional incentive. This should attract interest in your listing and increase the odds of unloading your contract in a timely manner. Once a match has been found, give your carrier a call and inquire about porting your phone number, if you wish to keep it.

If you are unable to find someone to take over your contract, you may want to consider breaking it and paying the early termination fees. Although this may be a hard loss to swallow, you can expect to make this money back within six months and reap substantial savings in the long run.

Save Additional Money on Your Cell Phone Bill

Regardless of your cell phone plan, there are a few steps you can take to lower your monthly bill. One suggestion is to drop cell phone insurance if you are currently paying for this service. Cell phone insurance tends to run five to ten dollars per month and usually carries a deductible of around one hundred dollars. Even if you have a high-end fancy device, it shouldn't cost more than the deductible to replace it with a comparable refurbished model.

Another easy way to save money on your cell phone bills is to avoid making international calls directly through your carrier. Fantastic international phone cards are readily available online that have rates as low as a few cents per minute. Many of these calling cards now offer pinless dialing from any phone number that you register with your account. Pingo.com, CallingCards.com, and SpeedyPin.com are three of the leading websites offering reasonably priced phone cards with this user-friendly feature.

Similarly, unless your plan includes free calls to 411, don't throw away your money by using this service. Instead of paying a couple dollars for each 411 call, you can get free directory assistance at 1-800-FREE411. You can call this toll-free number from any cell phone or landline in the country.

The only disadvantage to calling 1-800-FREE411 is that you'll have to listen to about ten seconds of advertisements before obtaining the phone number you requested. All in all, this is a reasonable trade-off compared to the ridiculous charges to which you would subject yourself otherwise.

Never Buy Accessories from Your Cell Phone Provider

The same overpriced cell phone accessories that carriers sell can typically be found on independent e-commerce sites for half the price. This includes items such as Bluetooth headsets, chargers, and mobile cases. If you want the exact models that your carrier offers, note down their brand names and model numbers and then compare prices on Amazon.com and eBay.com.

If you are open to buying similar accessories made by different manufacturers, visit Amazon.com and look over the consumer ratings and reviews in the accessory category that interests you. Amazon contains more consumer product reviews than any other website and has a great security system in place to ensure reviewer integrity. This system begins by allowing customers to leave product reviews only after they have created an account with Amazon and made a purchase. Because making a purchase on Amazon requires customers to have a credit card on file, there's instant third-party verification that they are who they claim to be.

HOME PHONES

Get VoIP Home Phone Service

The price for home phone service has come down substantially in the last few years. Not everyone wants or requires a home phone, but some of us do. If you fall into this group, voice over Internet protocol (VoIP) phone systems provide good opportunities to save money without compromising your service.

In layman's terms, VoIP means talking on the phone through your Internet connection. The better VoIP providers use an adapter to connect the phone directly to your Internet signal, eliminating the need to turn on your computer. In fact, these VoIP systems have nothing to do with your computer because your phone is directly hooked up to your Internet modem. Instead of placing calls through a landline, you will simply be making them through the Internet.

Almost all VoIP providers offer unlimited local and long-distance calling. In addition, standard home phone features, including voicemail, caller ID, call waiting, and three-way calling, are included in basic VoIP plans. In most situations you can keep your current phone number, and typically, a contract is not required. Unfortunately, you need to have a high-speed Internet connection to use VoIP service. However, I would recommend investing in high-speed Internet regardless because the Internet can help you save money in so many areas.

The only major drawback to getting VoIP service is that you would not be able to make or receive calls in the event of a power outage. As a result, if you live in a part of the country that experiences extreme weather, you may be better off sticking with traditional landline service. Otherwise, VoIP plans are a great option to consider.

Most major telecom providers now offer VoIP service. Typically, these plans start at twenty dollars per month and include unlimited nationwide calling and use of the provider's adaptor. While these rates are not bad, an even better option is to buy your own VoIP adaptor from one of a handful of companies that charge next to nothing for basic service. Ooma is the most popular company of this nature. Its adaptor currently costs around $120, but after buying it you will get free nationwide calling as well as most standard home phone features. The only charge for which you will be responsible is approximately $4.00 per month for service taxes. Ooma has been in business since 2007 and has a solid business model, dismissing fears of the company going out of business in the near future. Most consumers find their call quality to be identical to landline service, making this a good long-term investment that can save you hundreds of dollars a year.

If you find the cost of Ooma's hardware too hard to swallow, consider buying an Obihai VoIP adaptor. Obihai's

VoIP technology is nearly identical to Ooma's and far superior to the hardware offered by similar companies such as MagicJack and netTALK. Obihai's most recent model, the OBi202, has received great consumer reviews and only costs about sixty dollars.

The only major drawback to the OBi202 is that you must set it up with Google Voice or a similar VoIP application. Currently Google does not charge anything for unlimited nationwide calling, but some time in the future, this may change. Even if this does change, though, it's unlikely Google would charge more than ten dollars a month for its service.

It's worth mentioning that Google Voice does not allow you to call 911 directly. Although this may be a major concern, most 911 dispatch centers also have ten-digit phone numbers. After locating this number with the help of a search engine, you could always save it to your speed dial in case of an emergency.

Consider Using Your Cell Phone Exclusively

More and more consumers are canceling their home phone service and strictly using cell phones. Depending on your cell phone plan and your specific needs, canceling home service may be an option worth considering. If you decide to drop your home phone but tend to get bad cell phone coverage in your house, you may want to look into buying a femtocell. This device improves your call quality by transmitting a signal booster from a small base that can be kept anywhere in your home. Femtocells currently cost about two hundred dollars, but they will likely come down in price in the near future.

INTERNET AND PAY-TV

Compare Service Packages

There's an endless list of Internet providers and a multitude of ways to deliver Internet access, including cable, DSL, fiber optic, satellite, and dial-up systems. Generally speaking, Internet speed is the only thing with which you need to concern yourself. Because many of the saving methods in this book are tied to the Internet, I strongly suggest getting a high-speed connection. Typically, this will cost you around thirty to fifty dollars per month. If this is out of your budget, look into other Internet options. Just be sure to do in-depth research, as the quality of service can vary dramatically.

Your options for pay-TV are a little simpler. Just about every major telecom provider offers television service through cable, satellite, or fiber optic systems. Although each type of service has distinct features, they are all fairly similar for most of our needs.

If you currently have a contract for Internet or pay-TV service, you are probably better off riding it out and then utilizing the following suggestions. If you are not in a contract, you should be able to reduce your monthly rates by about 20 percent. The first step toward accomplishing this goal is to compare different service packages from a variety of telecom providers.

Typically, getting high-speed Internet and pay-TV service from the same provider will be the most inexpensive and convenient option. Providers of this sort usually promote their deals through the mail, radio, and television, so you should already be aware of the companies servicing your area. To get an idea of their current rates, visit their websites or give them a call.

If you are unhappy with your current service, disconnect it and take the best offer you can find. Otherwise, record the details of the best package available, take a few deep breaths, and get ready to engage in old-fashioned negotiation.

Renegotiate Your Monthly Payments

All service providers share the philosophy that keeping a customer is easier than trying to find a new one. As a result, any major Internet and pay-TV provider will have a revenue retention team. This team is strictly dedicated to retaining customers who are dissatisfied with their service and ready to cancel it. Generally, retention team members get incentives or bonuses based on their rate of success in placating customers. This works to your advantage because their goal is inevitably the same as yours—to keep you satisfied with their rates and service.

To speak to the retention team, you must call your telecom provider and tell them you want to cancel your service. Ultimately, this statement is nothing more than a way to get to the negotiating table. Think of it as a poker face in a game of cards. In the rare case that the provider calls your bluff, you can always find an excuse to terminate the call. Your service will never actually be canceled unless you give your service provider a cancellation date.

Before you call your telecom provider, make sure you have the best offer from a competitor in front of you. Also, try to recall how long you have had service with them. Your leverage will be stronger if you have been a customer for at least a year and have rarely been late with your payments.

Regardless of the company you are calling, your phone call should begin with a series of recorded prompts. At the appropriate prompt, say that you want to cancel your service. This should get your phone call transferred to the revenue retention team following a brief hold. After the retention team member introduces herself, you should once again state that you want to discontinue your service. When the team member asks you why you want to terminate service, say that their rates are too expensive and that you have received a more reasonable offer from a competitor. Stating that the provider's charges are too expensive will send a clear message that you want lower rates and not a discounted service upgrade.

When you are asked about the offer you received, you should provide the competitor's name and the basic package details. Despite how the retention team member responds to this, stand your ground. Tell the representative that you will be forced to cancel your service if she is unwilling to offer you comparable rates. While getting this point across, try to be as respectful and friendly as possible. Being pushy and rude will likely work against you in this type of situation.

After this dialogue, the retention team member will probably have a few subpar suggestions that involve different types of service downgrades. Politely decline her recommendations and tell her that you would like to move forward with the cancellation process. In most cases this will force her hand and lead to an offer that lowers your monthly payments significantly. This will typically be a six-month introductory or promotional package. However, as long as it does not include a contract, you should be able to maintain similar rates by repeating this process right before it expires.

If you happen to get someone on the phone who is unwilling to help you, tell the retention team member that you will call later with a specific cancellation date. Then, after hanging up the phone, call back and repeat this process with another representative. If that representative is also unwilling to adjust your rates, you may want to think about taking the more appealing deal you found. Being loyal to a telecom provider that is charging you more for less does not make sense from any angle.

Maintain Promotional Rates

Assuming you are successful in renegotiating your rates, you then want to make sure you maintain them. To accomplish this goal, it's important to keep track of when your promotional rates expire. You can do this by recording these dates in a calendar or daily planner. Then, call your service provider a few days before the rates are scheduled to change and repeat the process outlined previously.

Even if the provider is unwilling to keep you on the same promotional rate plan, the retention team will likely find another way to keep your monthly bill in the same ballpark without downgrading your service. Typically, service packages run in six-month cycles, requiring a phone call twice a year. All in all, this is not a bad trade-off for the hundreds of dollars you are likely to save annually.

SideStep Rental Charges

An additional way to bring down your telecom bills is to purchase hardware that you would normally rent from Internet and pay-TV providers. You can buy things like an Internet modem and router on Amazon or eBay for about the same cost as a six-month rental. Although buying your own hardware requires that you lay out a bit of money, in the long run, it should save you fifty to one hundred dollars a year for each device that you purchase. When buying these items, just be sure to get universal models so you have the freedom to change service providers whenever you desire.

Become a Seasonal Subscriber

Most consumers don't realize just how easy it is to drop and add premium channels. If you subscribe to a premium channel for a particular series that only runs for part of the year, cancel your subscription when the season ends, and then reinstate right before it starts up again. Likewise, if you want to watch a seasonal sport, upgrade your service package during the season, and then drop down to a more reasonable service package once it's over. Adding and dropping premium channels can be accomplished in a few minutes without any fees or headaches. In fact, if you drop certain channels seasonally, you may end up getting cheaper introductory rates when you reinstate them later on.

You can use this same strategy with online streaming and DVD rental companies like Netflix and Hulu Plus. If possible, when you reinstate your plan, use a different e-mail address and credit card number. Doing this should get you one free month of service.

Taking advantage of a few of these suggestions should reduce your telecom bills on numerous fronts. Keep in mind that unlike saving money on a single purchase, when you save money on your monthly expenses, you reap the benefits throughout the year.

HOW MUCH MONEY CAN YOU SAVE ON TELECOM SERVICES?

Saving method	Average savings
Getting wireless service from an MVNO	40% compared to plans from Verizon, AT&T, T-Mobile, and Sprint
Getting home phone service from Ooma	90% compared to plans from major telecom companies
Renegotiating your Internet and pay-TV rates	20% less than your current rates
Buying a modem, instead of renting one	$7 per month; $84 annually

CHAPTER TWO

INSURANCE

You probably have at least one or two insurance policies that aren't provided by your employer, such as auto, home, or life insurance. Although each of these policies has different factors that affect its premiums, the following suggestions should help you save money on all of them.

AUTO, HOME, AND LIFE INSURANCE

Raise Your Deductibles

Raising insurance deductibles makes good financial sense for most consumers. Unless you have already done this, your current polices probably cover any kind of loss over a couple hundred dollars. While having this kind of protection may provide psychological relief, due to high premiums, it's unlikely to save you money even if you have a minor claim.

How much you should raise your deductibles depends on your financial situation. For average middle-class Americans, raising auto deductibles up to five hundred dollars should be acceptable. If your current auto deductible is only a few hundred dollars, making this adjustment should lower your premium by about 20 percent. Because only one in every fifteen drivers makes an auto claim each year, doing this is likely to pay off, as long as you have good driving habits. With homeowner's or renter's insurance, consider even higher deductibles—just make sure you have enough money set aside to cover the deductible if the need arises.

Avoid Submitting Claims for Minor Damage

Submitting any claim for home or auto repairs will affect your claims history and result in higher premiums for many years to come. Insurers share information related to claims through an extensive database called CLUE (Comprehensive Loss Underwriting Exchange). Information stays in CLUE for five years from the time it was entered, which translates to five years of higher premiums. The best way to stay out of CLUE and other insurance databases is to handle the small stuff yourself. This step goes hand in hand with raising your deductibles.

If you would like to view your claim history, visit

PersonalReports.LexisNexis.com. Like credit reports, consumers are entitled to one free copy of their CLUE report annually.

Drop Coverage That You Don't Need

Most of us have coverage that we would be better off dropping altogether. A good example of this is collision and comprehensive coverage on a car of low value. If you have an automobile that's worth two thousand dollars or less, it's a good idea to buy only liability coverage. If you are unsure of the current value of your vehicle, you can get a fairly accurate assessment of it for free at Kelly Blue Book's website, KBB.com.

Along the same lines, if you are one of the few Americans who still have investment life insurance, consider canceling it and getting a term life policy. Investment life insurance usually has built-in fees and a poor rate of return, and it tends to be extremely confusing. Term life insurance, conversely, is simple, is relatively inexpensive, and does exactly what life insurance should do—it replaces the missing income of the person who died. Investing money is great, but doing it through your life insurance policy rarely pays off.

Consider Changing Insurance Providers

The insurance industry is extremely competitive. Consequently, if you invest a little time shopping around, you may be able to get coverage from more reliable insurers while reducing your premiums. In most states you can cancel your current insurance policies at any time and are legally entitled to a prorated refund. In some cases you may have to pay a cancellation fee, but usually even this is prohibited.

Amica Mutual, State Farm, and USAA are three of the best insurers to consider for auto, homeowner's, and renter's policies. As a result of their superb customer service and claims handling, they have been top performers in almost every Consumer Reports and JD Power insurance survey for the past several years. In addition, each has an A.M. Best financial strength rating of A++, the highest rating available.

Among these three insurers, State Farm services the widest variety of consumers. Generally, State Farm will insure just about anyone. Amica Mutual tends to be a bit pickier about its customers but should offer you great policies if you have a good credit score, driving record, and claims history. Unfortunately, USAA only offers coverage to military families. However, if you, your spouse, or one of your parents has served in the military, USAA's rates and service will be hard to beat.

While comparing auto quotes, you may also want to contact GEICO. Typically, GEICO has the most competitive rates for auto insurance. Although their customer service isn't the greatest, because auto claims are fairly straightforward, they should be pleasant enough to deal with if you have an accident.

If you are interested in comparing quotes for life insurance, your best option is to do in-depth research on insurers in your state. Unlike auto and home insurance, many of the best life insurance policies are available only in certain parts of the country. The website for your state's insurance department can be a great resource during this process. On its web page you should be able to find a consumer complaint ratio for each licensed insurer in the state. This ratio tells you how many customers were satisfied or dissatisfied when they filed claims with the insurance company in question. Although different states use different formulas for this equation, in general, insurers with the lowest ratios have had the smallest percentage of complaints filed against them.

Ask for Discounts

When you are collecting insurance quotes, be sure to inquire about potential discounts. Although most insurers offer a number of discounts, they will rarely tell you about them unless you ask. For example, auto and home insurance discounts might be available if you have added safety or security features, whereas life insurance discounts may be an option if you don't smoke or have normal blood pressure. Members of certain groups, such as AAA, AARP, and trade unions, often qualify for deductions. Even certain factors, such as having good grades if you are a student or taking a driving safety class, can lower auto premiums.

In addition, also look into bundle discounts. If you buy multiple policies from the same insurer, you should save money on all of your premiums.

PROTECTION PLANS

Protection plans are often promoted by banks and credit card companies. The most common form of shady insurance offered by these organizations is identity theft protection. Although identity theft is a legitimate concern, these plans provide little if any protection and recovery from this horrible form of theft. First of all, you should know that in most cases the companies offering identity theft insurance are often the same organizations failing to correctly protect your personal information. In addition, identity theft insurance usually does not reimburse any money that may be stolen from you. Although some policies may cover legal fees, in reality, a lawyer is almost never required to resolve an identity theft case. About the only useful aspect of identity theft insurance is the credit reports they send out periodically. While this information is useful, it's not worth shelling out fifteen dollars a month for it. A better alternative would be to take advantage of the free credit reports to which everyone is entitled annually. You can acquire these reports in less than five minutes from the federally sanctioned website AnnualCreditReport.com.

Price protection plans are another scam on which a number of companies are capitalizing. Like identity theft protection, it's highly unlikely that this bogus form of insurance will ever do anything but cost you money. Organizations love to create new ways to get monthly payments out of us, and as long as we keep falling for their schemes, who can blame them?

HOW MUCH MONEY CAN YOU SAVE ON INSURANCE?

Saving method	Average savings
Raising auto insurance deductibles from $250 to $500	20% on auto insurance premiums
Raising home insurance deductibles from $500 to $1,000	15% on home insurance premiums
Taking advantage of insurance discounts	5% on insurance premiums
Comparing insurers and switching policies if better coverage is found	15% on insurance premiums

CHAPTER THREE

HOME ENERGY

There are a number of ways to reduce your energy consumption. Unfortunately, most of these strategies involve sacrificing your personal comfort or investing significant amounts of money and time for a very small return. The following steps will help you avoid these pitfalls while significantly lowering your utility bills.

HEATING AND COOLING EXPENSES

Manage Your Thermostat

Heating and cooling expenses are the primary villains behind high utility bills in the United States. The most effective way to reduce this expense is to find the most suitable thermostat settings for your home. During winter months, most families find 68 degrees to be a good routine setting to use. If you're currently heating your home at a higher temperature, this is probably a good setting to try out for a few days. If this temperature seems a little too cool, try increasing your thermostat by one degree every day until you find a comfortable setting.

After finding a good thermostat setting to use during the day, you will want to figure out comfortable adjustments to make before going to bed and when you're away from home. Lowering the temperature by five degrees at night should go unnoticed when you're in bed and under your blanket. Likewise, when nobody is going to be home, you can generally lower your thermostat by ten degrees without causing discomfort when you return. If your house is too cold when you first get home or during the night, try raising the temperature by one degree each day until you find a setting that suits you and your household. As you go through this process, keep in mind that you will save roughly 3 percent on your heating costs for each degree you reduce. That being said, don't subject yourself to temperatures that are below your comfort level. The idea is to avoid wasting money by overheating your home, not to sit on your couch shivering.

To help members of your household remember your routine settings, put a dot with an ultra-fine-point marker above the three temperatures you will be using on each thermostat dial in your home. This should help keep everyone on track. When adopting this practice, keep in mind that all your efforts will be neutralized if you increase the temperature to 80 degrees when you first wake up. Wildly cranking up your thermostat won't heat your home any quicker and will only waste your money.

During the summer months, you can adopt a similar strategy for lowering cooling costs. Most families are comfortable setting their air-conditioning thermostat to 75 degrees when they are at home and increasing it by five degrees before leaving the house. Adopting the practice of closing drapes, curtains, or blinds during hot summer days can also help lower your cooling costs by preventing hot sunlight from entering your home.

To make temperature control easier, you may want to invest in a programmable thermostat. These devices allow you to preset the times you want to adjust your heating or cooling system so you have the luxury of waking up in the morning and returning home from work to a warm or cool house. Most programmable thermostats can store a week's worth of settings, while allowing you the freedom to do manual overrides whenever you like. Models made by Lux and Honeywell receive the best and most consistent consumer reviews. You can buy one of their basic seven-day programmable thermostats for around fifty dollars on Amazon and eBay.

Change Your Filters Often

Replacing or cleaning your filters regularly is one of the best ways to help your heating and cooling system run efficiently. Each type of filter comes with specific manufacturer's timelines for changing or cleaning. Sticking to these timelines will help ensure that your airflow does not become restricted and will save you money by reducing the energy needed to heat or cool your home.

When it comes to selecting a filter, a mid-range pleated filter is a good energy-efficient choice. These filters are reasonably priced, allow good airflow, and trap the majority of dust and allergens in the air. Ultra-inexpensive fiberglass filters allow air to flow freely, but they only catch about 10 percent of the dust that passes through their screens. On the other end of the spectrum, high-priced HEPA filters do a fantastic job of blocking dust and allergens but restrict airflow in a manner that could be bad for your furnace and your wallet.

Seal Air Leaks

Preventing air leaks in your home is the last key step to reducing heating and cooling costs. Air leaks allow hot and cool air to escape your home freely, costing you outrageous amounts of money. While this step primarily relates to heating costs, certain habits, such as closing doors to unused rooms, can reduce wasted energy any time of the year.

During the winter, one of the most effective ways to

reduce air leaks is to seal older windows and glass patio doors. The easiest way to do this is to buy insulation kits specifically designed for this task or weather stripping caulk like Dap Seal 'N Peel.

Fireplaces are also a major source of air leaks. Surprisingly, burning a fire in your fireplace sucks out more heat from your home than it produces. If you enjoy the ambience of a fire, either reduce your thermostat to 50 degrees or turn it off while your fire is burning. In addition, when you are not burning a fire, make sure the fireplace damper is closed.

Don't concern yourself with other places in your home where minor air leaks may occur. Putting draft stoppers under bedroom doors and foam gaskets under electrical sockets would only save you a few dollars each year. This kind of money isn't worth anyone's time and effort.

APPLIANCES

Lower the Thermostat Setting on Your Water Heater

Adjusting the thermostat setting on your water heater is another easy way to save money. Surprisingly, lowering this temperature will probably go completely unnoticed by family members. Initially, try adjusting it to 120 degrees. If this reduction causes any discomfort, slowly increase the temperature until you find a setting that doesn't bother anyone in your home. If you have a gas water heater, it may not display a temperature setting and instead have general descriptive marks such as "very hot," "hot," and "warm." Try setting this kind of thermostat somewhere between "warm" and "hot," and adjust it until you find an ideal temperature. You can usually access a water heater's thermostat by removing a metal plate on the front of it with a screwdriver.

It's worth mentioning that there's an extremely small risk of promoting legionella bacteria if your water heater is maintained at 120 degrees. If someone in your home has a suppressed immune system or a chronic respiratory condition, you may want to set your thermostat at 140 degrees as a precautionary measure. However, for the majority of the population, 120 degrees is considered a perfectly safe temperature for water heating.

After adjusting the temperature on your water heater, consider adding insulation to it. The easiest way to determine whether your water heater needs insulation is to touch it. If it's warm, it could use insulation. A simple way to insulate your water heater is to buy a precut water heater jacket. This should only cost about ten to twenty dollars. If you have a gas water heater, installing a water heater jacket can be more complicated. When this is the case, skip this step or have a qualified contractor install it the next time you are having work done in your home.

Clean Your Clothes Efficiently

Your washer and dryer probably consume more energy than any other appliance in your home. A good first step to using these machines more efficiently is to wash and dry full loads of clothes whenever possible. When you need to do a small load, make sure you at least adjust the load size dial to the appropriate setting. Also, it's important not to overwash your garments. Premature washing not only runs up utility bills but tends to shorten the life of your clothes. While these suggestions may sound like no-brainers, it's estimated that we all waste thousands of gallons of water each year by not abiding by them.

Surprisingly, heating water accounts for 90 percent of the energy your washing machine consumes. Keeping this in mind, you should try to use hot water only when necessary. Although linens, towels, and white garments may need to be washed in hot water, the rest of your laundry can be washed in warm or cold water.

When drying your clothes, be sure to clean the lint filter before running each load. Doing this will improve air circulation and allow your clothes to dry more quickly. Although it's best to run the dryer with full loads, try not to mix heavier clothes with lightweight clothes. Drying things like towels separately will enable you to run your machine for shorter periods of time when you are drying thinner garments. Along the same lines, try not to overdry your clothes.

If your dryer does not have a built-in moisture sensor, don't just set it for the maximum time, as most loads tend to dry long before their cycles end.

Wash Your Dishes Without Wasting Money

The easiest way to cut down on the amount of power your dishwasher consumes is to use its air-dry mode instead of its heated drying cycle. As with your clothing washer, also be sure to run your dishwasher with full loads. Filling up your dishwasher throughout the day is the best way to do this. If your dishwasher still isn't full at the end of the day, run the rinse cycle and then turn it off. This will allow you to keep dishes in your machine overnight without food particles hardening on them.

A lot of hot water waste can occur before you load your dishes into the dishwasher. Most of us tend to run hot water continually while we are scraping off food from our dishes. With a little effort, you should be able to scrape food particles off your dishes with a minimal amount of warm water.

It's also worth noting that unless you only have a handful of dishes, it's never more energy efficient to do them by hand. In fact, according to the California Energy Commission, washing your dishes in the dishwasher uses 37 percent less water than washing them yourself.

Save Additional Money in the Kitchen

One of the best ways to reduce energy expenses in the kitchen is to use small appliances to reheat or cook small meals. Using a microwave or a toaster oven not only uses less energy than your stove but also cooks your food more quickly and can help reduce cooling costs in the summer by generating less heat. When you are using stove burners, do your best to match up the pot size to the burner size. Using a pot that is too big or too small for a burner can waste 40 percent of its heat, and it won't warm your food any faster.

You can also improve the efficiency of your refrigerator if you take a few minutes to clean its coils every few months. Typically, these coils are located on the bottom of the refrigerator or under a protective guard on its backside. The easiest way to clean your refrigerator coils is to vacuum them with the wand attachment on your vacuum cleaner. If you are having difficulty getting all the dirt up with your vacuum wand, you can always buy a coil brush for a few dollars.

LIGHTING AND ELECTRONICS

Replace Standard Lightbulbs

Replacing standard lightbulbs with compact fluorescent lights (CFLs) is another simple way to lower your electric bill. CFLs use 75 percent less energy than standard bulbs and last about three times longer. The Department of Energy estimates that you will save forty dollars during the lifespan of each CFL in use. Multiply that by the number of lightbulbs in your home, and you should have a savings of about four hundred dollars.

The number one complaint with CFLs is that they are not bright enough. If this is a concern, buy bulbs with more lumens. Ideally, standard sixty-watt bulbs should be replaced with CFLs that produce a minimum of eight hundred lumens. You can find CFLs of this nature at Home Depot, Lowe's, Costco, Ace Hardware, and Amazon.com for as little as two dollars per bulb. CFLs do contain mercury, so they should not be thrown in the trash. Instead, you can drop off your used bulbs at a number of retail locations, including Home Depot, Lowe's, and IKEA.

Another energy-efficient option is to replace standard bulbs with LEDs (light-emitting diodes). LEDs use even less energy than CFLs and can last for decades. Also, these bulbs tend to be brighter than CFLs and do not contain mercury, so you won't have to go out of your way to dispose of them. LEDs currently cost upward of ten dollars for a sixty-watt replacement. However, over the next few years, they should come down in price, making them a good alternative to consider.

Eliminate Phantom Loads

Phantom loads, or *leaking electricity*, also contribute to high utility bills. These terms refer to the power that electrical devices continue to draw after they are switched off. According to the US Department of Energy, up to 75 percent of the energy drawn by electronic devices, such as televisions, computers, and kitchen appliances, occurs after they are turned off. You can eliminate this waste of electricity by unplugging small kitchen appliances after using them and by investing in energy-efficient power strips for your home entertainment and computer systems.

The most popular energy-efficient power strip has one master outlet that works in sync with a number of special outlets. When the device that is plugged into the master outlet is turned off, all of the special outlets stop consuming electricity. This type of power strip works well if you have a master device in your home entertainment and computer system. If you don't, consider getting a power strip with remote control. Remotely operated power strips allow you to stop phantom loads for numerous devices simply by flicking a switch. Both models usually include a few outlets that always draw power for electronic accessories that need to remain on, like an Internet modem or a DVR recorder. They also generally have built-in surge protectors for sensitive electronics. Belkin and Smart Strip are the two leading manufacturers specializing in energy-efficient power strips. You can purchase one of their models for twenty to fifty dollars on Amazon.com, eBay.com, and Newegg.com.

WATER CONSUMPTION

Consider Using a Low-Flow Showerhead

Using a low-flow showerhead will help reduce your water consumption as well as the energy it takes to heat your water. Most low-flow showerheads use about 40 percent less water than standard showerheads, allowing you to save money on two different expenses. Models made by Oxygenics, Delta, and American Standard receive the best consumer reviews and should only cost about thirty dollars.

On top of changing your showerhead, you might want to consider switching the faucet aerator on your bathroom sink to a low-flow model. Low-flow aerators use about 50 percent less water than standard models, which again will save you money on two different expenses. Niagara and Neoperl make good aerators that cost about five dollars apiece.

As far as your kitchen faucet is concerned, using a low-flow aerator probably isn't a good idea. Low-flow aerators can be a nuisance when you're trying to fill a cooking pot or water house plants. A better choice for your kitchen sink would be an aerator with a lever for adjusting water pressure. Most of these aerators also include the option of switching your water flow from a downpour to a spray. Adjustable kitchen sink aerators are sold at just about every hardware and home improvement store and are also readily available online.

Prevent Water Leaks

Water leaks tend to be most common in kitchen and bathroom faucets as well as toilet bowls. If you notice a water leak from a faucet, it most likely is due to a worn-out washer. New washers are inexpensive and can be replaced in a few minutes. If you have not done this chore before, visit the helpful website DoItYourself.com for detailed instructions.

The best way to check for toilet bowl leaks is to conduct a simple test. Remove the toilet bowl cover from the tank, and pour in a little food coloring or cold coffee. Avoid using the toilet for half an hour, and then check the bowl to see if the water has changed color. If there's any detectable change, you have a leak.

Replacing malfunctioning toilet bowl parts usually costs less than ten dollars and is very easy to do. Again, DoItYourself.com can help you with this task. Of course, if you are a renter, calling your landlord and asking him to fix any visible leaks is the easiest and least expensive option.

Similarly, if you don't have a low-flow toilet bowl, you can at least reduce the amount of water it uses by placing a one-liter bottle full of water in the tank. This bottle will replace one liter of water that your toilet bowl consumes each time you flush it. Although this doesn't sound like a lot of water, in the course of a year it could add up to thousands of gallons.

LONG-TERM ENERGY INVESTMENTS

Seal Ducts and Insulate Your Home

Sealing the ducts in your heating and cooling systems is the first big utility investment worth considering. The U.S. Environmental Protection Agency (EPA) estimates that in the average home, 20 percent of the air traveling through the duct system is lost owing to holes and leaks. These leaks can result in drastically higher utility bills and make it difficult to maintain comfortable temperatures in your home.

Many individuals opt to undertake this task themselves to avoid making what can be a very expensive investment. Typically, very little skill is required for duct sealing, and all that is usually needed is some free time and a willingness to crawl into tight spaces and get dirty. There's a great deal of free information related to this task online. Doing a little bit of research is the best way to decide if you're up to doing it yourself or prefer to hire a contractor. If you decide to hire a contractor, it's a good idea to set aside some time to compare service quotes. AngiesList.com and HomeAdvisor.com are good consumer review sites that can help you find reasonable and recommended help.

Insulating your attic floor (if you have an attic) and

insulating hot water pipes can also help lower heating and cooling costs. As these tasks can be a little more complicated to perform, you'll probably want to hire help. If you're feeling extremely ambitious and want to do them yourself, at least invest in a good guidebook. One of the more popular guidebooks that covers home insulation is Bruce Harley's *Insulate and Weatherize* (Taunton Press, 2012).

Buy Energy-Efficient Appliances

As a general rule of thumb, you are better off getting the full life out of your existing appliances before replacing them. That being said, when those appliances finally breathe their last breath, it makes good financial sense to buy energy-efficient replacements. The easiest way to ensure you are buying energy-efficient machines is to look for qualifying Energy Star models. If you have some free time, you may want to do more in-depth research on the most cost-effective appliances that meet these standards.

Despite what you may have read elsewhere, replacing your windows with energy-efficient frames is horrible advice to follow if you want to save money. New windows usually cost well over one thousand dollars, making it unlikely you will ever see a return on your initial investment. If you are replacing your windows for cosmetic reasons, then you might as well buy the energy-efficient units; otherwise, seal them during the winter.

Before concluding this section, it's worth mentioning that the simplest way to reduce the cost of your utility bills is to avoid wasting energy and water unnecessarily. Leaving lights on in rooms that nobody is using or forgetting to turn your stereo off can add up to substantial amounts of money over time. Likewise, many of us still brush our teeth and shave with the water running, not only throwing away money but also showing little regard for the environment. With a little focus and determination you should be able to overcome these lazy routines, if you haven't already.

HOW MUCH MONEY CAN YOU SAVE ON HOME ENERGY BILLS?

Saving method	Average savings
Using recommended thermostat settings	20% of annual heating and cooling expenses
Sealing air leaks in your home during winter months	10% of annual heating and cooling expenses
Lowering the thermostat on your water heater	10% of annual water heating expenses
Replacing standard lightbulbs with CFLs or LEDs	75% of annual home lighting expenses
Using energy-efficient power strips for entertainment devices	100% of leaking electricity per device

CHAPTER FOUR

GROCERY SHOPPING

You are probably familiar with some of the common strategies for saving money on groceries. Most of these routines involve cutting out and filing coupons, looking through a variety of circular flyers, and finally, matching your coupons with items that are on sale. If you are looking for a time-consuming hobby, this is a great approach to consider. Many members of my family are as passionate as stock investors when it comes to their coupon filers and the amount of money they have saved them. The biggest advantage to this strategy is that money will undoubtedly be saved. The disadvantages include the amount of time these activities consume and a drastic reduction in your product selection.

If you are not comfortable making these kinds of sacrifices, there are other painless ways to save money on groceries. Below are a number of suggestions that should reduce the cost of your favorite products.

GROCERIES

Buy Fresh Produce at Reduced Rates

Most people agree that the cornerstone to a healthy diet is fresh fruits and vegetables. Fresh produce is more expensive than canned or frozen goods, but investing in our health is perhaps the most important investment we can make. The best way to reduce your grocery bills and still load up on fresh greens is to shop for fruits and vegetables at produce markets.

Produce markets are typically small, open-air stores dedicated to fruits and vegetables. The prices at these markets tend to be 30 to 50 percent less than at traditional grocery stores. These stores are in a position to offer such discounts because of their buying strategies and lower overhead costs. Generally, produce markets buy items in much larger quantities than grocery stores and often buy and sell ultra discounted items that are already ripe. The produce that these markets purchase usually comes off the same trucks and is from the same growers that supply traditional grocery stores. The only difference is that its shelf life is typically a few days shorter. Consequently, it's important to be extra selective, especially if you don't plan to eat all of the items you are buying within a couple of days. Taking a few extra moments to inspect and dig through the produce is the best way to ensure that you are getting quality fruits and vegetables at great rates.

Along the same lines, many Asian markets have good prices on produce. Like produce markets, Asian markets have lower overhead costs and buy in bulk, which allows them to pass along substantial savings to consumers. Although these markets tend to have a stronger focus on traditional Asian vegetables and fruits, most of them also offer a reasonable selection of American produce staples.

Unfortunately, at both produce and Asian markets, quality and pricing can vary dramatically from one location to the next. The easiest way to find a market that offers both of these important qualities is to visit a consumer review website. For this particular business model, Yelp.com is a great website to consult. Yelp is the most widely used consumer review website to date and covers any and every kind of business. Anyone can submit a review on Yelp, and currently more than thirty million consumers have done so. To create a reliable infrastructure, Yelp uses an automated review filter that helps eliminate owner-manipulated and malicious reviews. While it's true that some biased and fake reviews occasionally slip through the cracks, it should be easy to spot these kinds of comments and identify them for what they are.

To begin your search on Yelp, enter the city in which you live, along with a general business description such as "cheap produce." Running a query of this type will not only bring up produce and Asian markets but will also include grocery stores that have a reputation for selling fruits and vegetables for reasonable rates. To simplify things, Yelp displays the average consumer rating next to each listing as well as the number of reviews each business has received. After looking over this information and reading through a handful of reviews, you should be able to put together a decent list of markets in your local area.

If you're looking for reasonably priced organic produce, try to buy as many items as you can in prepackaged bags. Prebagged produce staples, such as carrots, potatoes, onions, garlic, apples, oranges, and lemons, are typically about 50 percent cheaper than the exact same items sold by the pound. You should be able to find a good selection of prepackaged organic fruits and vegetables at any larger health food store.

Join a Warehouse Club

Costco, Sam's Club, and BJ's Wholesale are the most common warehouse clubs in the United States. All of these chains should feature a number of your favorite grocery products in large wholesale sizes. In addition to packaged groceries, most of their locations also offer dairy, meat, seafood, produce, baked goods, pet food, and alcoholic beverages. Although buying large amounts of certain perishable items may be a concern, this shouldn't present a problem with many items you routinely purchase.

To keep their overhead costs as low as possible, most warehouse clubs have very basic layouts and no-frills merchandising. In addition, they typically have the lowest profit margins in the grocery industry. As a result of these business strategies, they are able to offer fantastic bargains that can't be found elsewhere.

A membership to one of these clubs costs about fifty dollars per year, making it an affordable investment for most of us. Routinely buying just two or three items from a warehouse club will typically cover your annual fees and then some. If, at any point in the year, you find that you are not saving as much money as expected, all of these chains will refund your membership fees in full.

Over the years, warehouse clubs have greatly expanded their range of products and services. Today, most locations still function primarily as a grocery club, while also offering electronics, cookware, clothing, pharmacies, and optical centers. Although some of these additional items and services may be a good value, their groceries usually provide the best opportunity for savings.

Buy Store-Brand Staples

After shopping at a grocery club, you will still need to shop at a traditional grocery store for some products. Ideally, you should shop at markets that offer a large selection of store-brand products. Unlike a decade ago, most store-brand products are now made by leading national brands. In many cases the only differences between these items and brand-name products are their logos and packaging.

Most grocery chains sell store brands far below their profit margins as loss leaders. Typically, these items will be dramatically cheaper than similar products, even when they're on sale. Store-brand products are particularly good choices for food staples such as cooking oils, canned beans, frozen vegetables, and milk and eggs. For other formulated items, such as boxed cereal, cookies, ice cream, condiments, and marinades, experiment with store brands when you feel compelled to do so. If these products don't live up to your expectations, you can always exchange them the next time you are in the store.

If you prefer buying natural and organic products, you should be able to find a decent selection of store-brand items at most health food chains as well as at some traditional grocery stores, such as Safeway. If you are looking for gourmet and specialty items, pay a visit to Trader Joe's. About 80 percent of the products sold at Trader Joe's are store-brand items that mainly fall under these categories.

Use Coupons That You Don't Have to Cut Out and Organize

If you are like most consumers, you are probably partial to a few brand-name products. The simplest way to save money on these items is to buy coupons for them online. Buying coupons online removes the headache of sorting through endless newspapers and flyers, while eliminating the need to cut out and file these tiny pieces of paper. When your coupons arrive in the mail, you can simply toss them into one big envelope because you will have only a handful of coupons for your favorite products.

Among the many websites selling coupons, eBay undoubtedly offers the biggest variety of choices. Besides popular national brands, eBay also features hundreds of coupons for natural and organic products. In fact, any coupon that is in print is probably available on eBay. The average price per coupon on eBay is around 10 percent of its value, but most coupons are strictly sold in quantities of five or more. As a result, it only pays to buy coupons for items that you don't mind stockpiling.

If you tend to buy more popular and traditional brands, you should also visit TheCouponClippers.com. Although this site does not have the diversity of coupons that eBay offers, it does have a decent selection and allows you the freedom to buy coupons in whatever quantities you fancy.

Other books and blogs recommend that their readers take advantage of the many websites offering free print-at-home coupons. If you are looking for an activity to pass the time, then go ahead and look through the myriad websites offering this service. However, I suspect you'll find this process disappointing. In addition to the time required to navigate these sites, their variety of coupons is very limited. My suggestion would be to spend your free time in better ways and skip this fruitless experience.

Take a Shopping List to the Grocery Store

Taking a shopping list to the grocery store can save you both time and money. To understand how this can be beneficial, it's important to understand how grocery stores profit from your business. Your typical markets lure you into their buildings with sale flyers that feature popular items at a great value. Like store-brand products, most of these items are loss leaders. After their flyers draw you into their stores, they then rely on their layout and merchandising to increase your planned basket size and turn a significant profit on your visit.

Almost every grocery store has the same layout. The dairy department is usually along the back wall because milk and eggs are two of the most commonly purchased grocery items. For shoppers to get a gallon of milk, they have to walk through the entire building, during which time they are likely to be lured into buying a number of other products. Likewise, the produce, meat, and seafood departments are typically found along the perimeter of the building, forcing shoppers to encounter a number of tempting items as they walk across the store. Finally, if their store merchandising fails to produce impulse purchases, every market makes one final attempt to increase their sales with tempting last-minute products at their cash registers.

Although most of us are aware of these marketing strategies, statistics show we still bite the bait at the end of their hooks. In fact, around 50 percent of the average shopper's purchases are impulse items. The majority of these products tend to be junk food and other treats that negatively affect our health on top of our finances. The best defense against this money-wasting ritual is to write a shopping list and stick to it whenever you visit a grocery store.

PAPER AND CLEANING PRODUCTS

Buy Paper and Cleaning Products in Bulk

Most of the paper and cleaning products that you routinely use should be available in an economy size. Besides warehouse clubs, superstores like Target and Wal-Mart now offer economy packs of toilet paper, paper towels, napkins, diapers, and detergents. Buying these items in bulk should not only save you money but will save you time and energy by reducing unnecessary shopping trips and emergency supply runs.

Other household products, such as plastic wrap, aluminum foil, sponges, and resealable food storage bags, are likely to be found in economy packs exclusively at warehouse clubs. If you have a warehouse club membership, remember to take an inventory of these items before shopping there.

The biggest challenge with buying paper and cleaning products in bulk is the limited storage space in our homes. If storage space is a concern in your house, plan to dedicate an hour to reorganizing a few cupboards or a closet. You will likely be amazed with how much space you can create with a little effort. Getting rid of old kitchen appliances and pots and pans that haven't been used in years is one of the easiest ways to create extra room. If parting with these items is a struggle for you, keep in mind that your attachment to them is indirectly costing you money.

Buying a few stackable plastic storage containers can also help create space. These containers are commonly sold at superstores, home improvement stores, and warehouse clubs. They cost about ten dollars per container, and typically two or three are enough to create plenty of room. The blog Unclutterer.com has further suggestions that may be useful in squeezing the most out of small spaces.

Visit Your Local Dollar Store

Dollar stores are good places to buy cleaning products when quality is not a top priority. Typically, all-purpose, surface, floor, window, and toilet bowl cleaners can be found for a dollar apiece at these saving outlets. Also, commonly bought items, such as greeting cards, gift wrap, scotch tape, and stationary supplies, are sold for unmatchable prices. Depending on where you live, you should have a number of dollar stores in your local area. As most of these stores offer a similar mix of items, it shouldn't matter which location you visit.

Make Simple Cleaning Solutions at Home

If you prefer to use natural household cleaners, making your own home solutions is a good option. A good universal cleaning solution can be made by mixing one part vinegar to one part water in a spray bottle. This works great as an all-purpose cleaner and can be used on windows and almost any surface in your home. This solution does have a vinegary scent, but it tends to disappear after a few minutes and does not leave a lingering odor.

When you need to clean your tub or bathroom sink, you can make a good natural cleaner with baking soda. The easiest way to do this is by mixing baking soda with a little bit of water to form a cleaning paste. Apply this paste it to your tub or sink and scrub away.

HOW MUCH MONEY CAN YOU SAVE ON GROCERIES?

Saving method	Average savings
Buying fruits and vegetables at produce markets	40% compared to standard retail pricing
Shopping at a warehouse club	30% compared to standard retail pricing
Buying store-brand staples	30% compared to brand-name products
Making simple cleaning solutions	70% compared to similar cleaners
Purchasing coupons online	90% of the coupons' value

CHAPTER FIVE

HEALTH AND BEAUTY PRODUCTS

Many frugal folks pride themselves on the amount of money they save on health and beauty products. By combining coupons, rebates, and sale items, thrifty shoppers routinely save large amounts of money on these products and, at times, even get them for free. Although on the surface this strategy sounds great, it actually bears the same bitter fruit as grocery couponing; a hefty investment of time and a lack of product selection.

If you are in a tight spot or are out to save as much money as you can, then it makes sense to combine rebates, sales, and coupons. However, if you are comfortable spending a little money to get the items you prefer, there are other good ways to save money on health and beauty products.

TOILETRIES AND COSMETICS

Buy Toiletries and Cosmetics Online

Buying toiletries and cosmetics in bulk will typically save you money. Although warehouse clubs and superstores tend to sell these items in economy sizes, chances are they won't feature many of your favorite brand-name products. When this is the case, look for them online.

Among the many websites that sell toiletries and cosmetics, eBay.com, Amazon.com, and Soap.com tend to have the strongest focus on bulk deals. All three of these sites sell thousands of popular products in multiple quantities. Locating these deals on Amazon.com and Soap.com is pretty straightforward, but finding them on eBay can be a little more time consuming. To make this process easier, try sorting your search results on eBay from highest priced to lowest priced. When you sort your search results in this fashion, all of the bulk deals will come up at the top of the list.

Buying in quantity will naturally cost you more money up front, but in the long run this strategy will save you loads of money. Because cosmetic and personal hygiene products have a tremendously long shelf life, you shouldn't think twice about purchasing a six-month or one-year supply of any product you regularly use.

Use the Correct Amount of Each Product

Perhaps the easiest way to save money on toiletries and cosmetics is to stop using excessive amounts of them. Without even thinking about it, most of us use twice the recommended amount of shampoo, toothpaste, deodorant, fragrances, and hair styling products. Due to the chemicals in some of these items, this practice can be harmful to your health as well as wasteful. By simply following the instructions on the packaging, you should be able to make each of these products last twice as long.

PRESCRIPTION AND OVER-THE-COUNTER MEDICINE

Switch to Generic Brands

Buying generic brands is the simplest way to save money on prescription and over-the-counter medicine. By law, generic medications are required to have the same active ingredients as their brand-name counterparts. Because the active ingredients are exactly the same, the only difference between the two products is found in their inactive ingredients and fillers. Despite this fact, brand-name drugs still cost up to 80 percent more than generic medication.

In the United States, drug patents are good for twenty years, but this clock starts ticking before clinical trials even begin. By the time a new drug is approved by the U.S. Food and Drug Administration and available for consumers, there's usually seven to twelve years left on the patent. As a result, most drugs that have been on the market for a while have generic counterparts.

Although generic replicas may not be available for newer drugs, similar generic products often are. If you are taking a drug that does not have a generic counterpart, do a little research and explore generic alternatives. After finding a few good options, compile a list of them to discuss with your doctor.

If there are not any generic replicas or alternatives available to use in place of your prescriptions, look into copay assistance programs. These programs are offered by pharmaceutical companies as a way to lower out-of-pocket expenses. Usually copay assistance programs are available to anyone regardless of their household income. If you wish to pursue this option, call the toll-free phone numbers associated with each of your brand-name prescriptions.

Don't Overpay for Your Prescriptions

Getting prescription drugs through mail-order programs tends to be the least expensive option for most medications. Usually these programs allow you to purchase your meds in a three-month supply for a discounted price. In addition to insurance providers, most Medicare plans also have a mail-order program that not only saves consumers money but also allows them the luxury of having their prescriptions delivered to their front door. To find out if this money-saving option is available, call your insurance or Medicare provider.

If you don't have prescription coverage, taking advantage of mail-order programs can still save you money. The popular website BidRx.com is a great place to explore your options when this is the case. This innovative website allows independent pharmacies the opportunity to bid for your business. After entering each of your prescriptions on BidRx, you will instantaneously receive a number of competitive offers from pharmacies around the country. Typically, the best deals on BidRx will be more economical than local pharmacy pricing.

Consider Additional Ways to Save Money

Another good way to save money on prescription drugs and other health-related expenses is to take advantage of a flexible spending account (FSA), if that option is available to you. Many businesses offer these plans as a way to help their employees save money on out-of-pocket medical expenses. Each year, you can elect a set dollar amount to go into this account as a pretax deduction. In addition to avoiding taxes on health care, taking advantage of this option will also lower your taxable income throughout the year.

The only downside to a FSA is that the money you put into it does not roll over from year to year. As a result, it's important to come up with the most accurate estimate you can for your out-of-pocket health expenses annually. If you need help with this task, use one of the many FSA calculators available online. Kiplinger.com has a good calculator that is thorough but not too complex.

If you have a health care plan with an annual deductible of at least $1,250 for single coverage or $2,500 for family coverage, you should also be eligible for a health savings account (HSA). A HSA is very similar to a FSA, but the money you put into it rolls over each year so that you are not up against a use-it-or-lose-it deadline. As with a retirement account, any money remaining in your HSA when you reach age sixty-five can be withdrawn without penalty. You can open a HSA at most banks and credit unions.

Both of these accounts can be used for a variety of expenses, including deductibles, copays, prescriptions, dental care, eyewear, chiropractic adjustments, and even acupuncture. If you are currently paying out of pocket for any of these things, give this option serious consideration.

One final way to save money on prescriptions is to buy your medication with double the prescribed strength and split your pills in half. Prescriptions drugs often cost the same amount of money regardless of the dosage, providing a nice additional way to lower medical costs. This isn't an option for all medications, but it can be done with many drugs. If your doctor permits you to do this, you can purchase a pill splitter for around five dollars at any pharmacy.

EYEWEAR

Save Money on Your Primary Glasses

In the past thirty years, the price of eyeglasses has tripled. This increase is primarily due to the world's largest eyewear company, Luxottica. Luxottica manufactures eyeglasses for most of the major brands on the market, including designer lines like Gucci, Ralph Lauren, DKNY, Burberry, Chaps, Ray Ban, and Oakley. In addition, Luxottica also owns the vision insurance provider EyeMed and major eyewear retail chains such as Lens Crafters, Pearl Vision, Sunglass Hut, Sears Optical, and Target Optical. As I am sure you guessed, almost all of the glasses sold at these stores are made by Luxottica and marked up to exorbitant prices.

Whether or not you have a vision plan, shopping at these stores is likely to cost you hundreds of dollars. The best way to avoid this expense is to shop at discount eyewear retailers that are not owned by Luxottica and do not sell glasses made by them. Costco, BJ's Optical, Sam's Club, and Wal-Mart are the major chains that fall into this category. At all of these stores you should be able to find a number of frames that are comparable to those made by Luxottica but that cost less than half the price.

Most discount chains accept very few insurance plans. However, after purchasing eyeglasses from an out-of-network provider, you may be able to get a partial reimbursement from your vision insurance provider. Be sure to inquire about this ahead of time and find out what proof of purchase you'll need to be reimbursed.

Another way to save money on eyeglasses is to get the lenses replaced in one of your existing frames. Should you need a new prescription, you can call the optometrists listed in your area and make an appointment with the least expensive one you can find. If this is not necessary, get in touch with the last optical shop where you bought a pair of glasses and have them fax you a copy of your prescription. By law they are required to pass this information on to you, and generally they will be more than happy to do so.

When you buy replacement lenses, don't make the mistake of going to an optical shop. Several reputable websites will replace eyeglass lenses for a fraction of the cost that retail stores charge. Of these sites, 39DollarGlasses.com is the most widely used. For thirty-nine dollars, this site will replace your old, single-vision lenses with new polycarbonate high-index lenses. These lenses are thin and lightweight and include 100 percent UVA and UVB protection, along with a scratch-resistant coating. In addition, if you want to add a glare-resistant coating, you can do so for just twenty-five dollars, instead of paying upward of seventy-five dollars at a retail store.

39DollarGlasses.com has been around for years and has been used by thousands of consumers. Although there have been complaints about shipping times taking longer than expected, the vast majority of consumers have been very satisfied with the quality of their lenses.

Get Inexpensive Backup Glasses

Believe it or not, you can now get a pair of basic prescription glasses for just seven dollars online. The two leading websites offering inexpensive eyeglasses are ZenniOptical.com and EyeBuyDirect.com. Both sites have numerous options starting at seven dollars for frames and single-vision lens. Although I wouldn't recommend using such glasses for your primary eyewear, they tend to work just fine as backups.

The only major drawback to buying glasses online is the inconvenience of having to have them adjusted after they arrive in the mail. However, most optical shops will not charge you anything for this service if you pretend to look around the store for a minute or two.

Another good resource for inexpensive glasses is the online blog GlassyEyes.blogspot.com. This blog is dedicated to finding discounted glasses at unbeatable prices and has helped numerous consumers do just that.

Save Money on Contact Lenses

E-commerce sites also tend to have the best bargains on contact lenses. A good rule of thumb to use when shopping for contacts is to buy them in bulk. Purchasing a year's supply at a time is usually a good choice. Among the websites offering the best bulk deals are 1800Contacts.com, Coastal.com, and VisonDirect.com.

You can also save money on contact lenses by talking to your eye doctor about switching to inexpensive alternative brands. Although some alternative brands should be avoided, others tend to be more or less identical to expensive brand-name options. If you find an alternative brand to be uncomfortable, the websites listed previously should refund your money on any unopened boxes that you purchased from them. Though you may lose a few dollars trying out different brands, in the long run, making this adjustment can save hundreds of dollars a year without any noticeable difference in your vision or comfort.

HOW MUCH MONEY CAN YOU SAVE ON HEALTH AND BEAUTY PRODUCTS?

Saving method	Average savings
Buying toiletries and cosmetics in bulk	30% compared to standard retail pricing
Buying generic prescriptions and over-the-counter medicine	30% compared to brand-name drugs
Buying prescription drugs through mail-order programs	15% compared to standard retail pricing
Buying eyewear from recommended retail stores and websites	50% compared to standard retail pricing

CHAPTER SIX

CLOTHING AND HOUSEHOLD ITEMS

It might surprise you to learn that the same brand-name clothing sold on the racks at Macy's and Dillard's is available for half the cost elsewhere. Likewise, top-of-the-line furniture and electronics can be found for discounted prices with ease. The following tips should help you save money on all these items without compromising the quality to which you are accustomed.

CLOTHING

Buy Selective Clothing Online

Each year more and more consumers are shopping for clothing online. Online shopping is not only more convenient than shopping at a department store but also offers good money-saving opportunities. To help consumers get comfortable with this idea, most websites selling clothing offer very lenient return policies. Typically you can return any garment that doesn't fit properly for a full refund within thirty days. In some cases, e-commerce sites will even pay for your return shipping if you are dissatisfied with your order. Although you may be wary of buying certain apparel online, you should at least feel comfortable purchasing clothing made by companies already represented in your wardrobe. In these situations you will know exactly what styles and sizes are an ideal fit.

Amazon and eBay undoubtedly offer the biggest selection of apparel. In fact, on both of these websites you should be able to find practically any garment you desire. For example, if you are looking for a pair of Levi's jeans, type that into either website's search bar, along with the gender, size, and style you want. After running your query, you should have a number of jeans to choose from that match all the criteria you entered.

Amazon's return policy allows you to return almost any apparel order for a full refund within thirty days. In addition, Amazon will pay for your return shipping on any items that are eligible for their Free Super Saver Shipping or Prime Shipping. Unfortunately, eBay allows individual sellers to set their own return policies, so you'll want to review these before making a purchase. However, thanks to eBay's Buyer

Protection Policy, any items that are not accurately described can be returned for a full refund.

If you are interested in secondhand clothing, eBay again has the largest inventory on hand. To help distinguish worn-out apparel from like-new items, look for clothing described as "gently used." This term implies that the garment is still in great condition, with few if any signs that it has been worn before.

For discounted high-end luxury apparel, Bluefly.com, Yoox.com, and members-only websites are all good options. Bluefly.com and Yoox.com function like most other e-commerce stores, but members-only websites operate a bit differently. This new breed of e-commerce site offers a limited number of items for a short period of time. Featured items tend to be offered for two or three days in what has become known as "boutiques" or "events." After each event ends, new items are available for a similar time frame.

Good members-only sites to visit include Gilt.com, BeyondtheRack.com, HauteLook.com, Ideeli.com, and Ruelala.com. When you explore these websites, try to avoid getting caught up in the hype they create with their short-lived sales. Do your best to disregard e-mails from them promoting boutiques and strictly visit their websites when you are looking to buy a particular item.

Shop at Off-Price Retailers

Off-price retailers are stores that sell popular brand-name items at discounted prices. The savings offered at these locations tend to be between 20 and 60 percent when compared to department stores. Stores in this retail sector are in a position to offer such deals as a result of their buying strategies. Typically off-price retailers buy their merchandise for next to nothing from large department stores and manufacturers looking to unload excess inventory. While some of these items are unfashionable clutter, the majority of their merchandise tends to be high-end and overstock clothing that simply didn't sell as well as forecasted.

Among the many off-price retail chains, Marshalls, T.J. Maxx, Ross, and Burlington Coat Factory consistently receive the best consumer reviews. Like most off-price retailers, all of these chains feature brand-name clothing, accessories, footwear, towels, linens, luggage, and kitchenware. On top of having a good variety of these items, each chain has done a good job of maintaining its own special niche. Marshalls has a strong focus on basic apparel and footwear and offers a broader selection of men's clothing than most of the other stores in this sector. T.J. Maxx has a great selection of apparel accessories and caters more to female clientele than the other chains. Ross has a good assortment of both men's and women's apparel but distinguishes itself from the pack with its variety of teen clothing. Burlington Coat Factory has the biggest stores in this sector, which offer a tremendous selection of basic apparel, coats, formal wear, bedding, home furnishings, and big and tall options. With a little luck, two or three of these chains will have stores in your local area.

If you are interested in off-price retailers featuring luxury and upscale clothing, see if there's a Stein Mart or Loehmann's nearby. Both these chains do offer basic apparel, though they tend to be higher-end versions of the other off-price retailers discussed.

When shopping at off-price retailers, try to be mindful of upcoming holidays and birthdays. Because their inventory changes so often, you never know what you are going to find. Equipping yourself with a list and planning ahead can save you time and energy in the future.

To keep prices as low as they do, off-price retailers tend to employ fewer staff than department stores. The major downside to this is that they are not as nicely laid out and organized, so you may have to spend more time digging through their merchandise. Although this can be a hassle, their deals should make up for it.

Take Advantage of Clothing Outlets

Clothing outlets don't offer as many bargains as off-price retailers, but their merchandise is generally less expensive than similar items in department stores. Perhaps the biggest advantages to visiting outlets is the array of clothing they offer and the freedom to get the specific brand names you desire.

Most clothing outlets are found on the outskirts of big cities and tend to be grouped together in mini-malls. Chelsea Premium Outlets and Tanger Outlets operate the largest networks of outlet centers, with a combined total of over one hundred locations in the United States. At these centers you can find outlets for a number of the most popular apparel brands in the business.

If you live near an outlet mall, it's certainly worth heading up there and seeing what it has to offer. However, try to avoid visiting these stores on weekends, when they tend to be packed with tourists.

Save Money at Department Stores

If you are partial to shopping at department stores, there are still ways to reduce your bill in an effortless fashion. The easiest way to do this is to buy discounted gift cards for the chains where you shop most often. Selling discounted gift cards has become a common way for individuals to turn unwanted gifts into hard cash. This trend started on eBay years ago and now has many websites solely dedicated to its cause.

Leading the pack of gift card exchange websites are Cardpool.com, GiftCardRescue.com, and MonsterGiftCard.com. On these websites consumers can buy gift cards for their favorite department and clothing stores for around 10 to 20 percent below their face value. Generally, you can find good gift cards throughout the year on these sites. However, if you are looking for hard-to-find gift cards, take advantage of the many individuals looking to sell them after the winter holidays. During this time of year you may even find discounted gift cards for off-price retailers and outlets.

Rent Apparel for Special Occasions

At some point in the year you will probably need a fancy outfit for a party or event. Formal attire for a special occasion can cost hundreds of dollars. As opposed to spending this kind of money over and over again or wearing the same outfit every time an event comes up, consider renting luxury apparel. On top of designer dresses and tuxedos, shoes, handbags, and jewelry can also be rented for a fraction of its cost. In addition, most clothing rental services offer dry cleaning and insurance for a small fee, so you need not worry if you happen to spill red wine all over your outfit.

For women's apparel, RentTheRunway.com is a great website to visit. RentTheRunway features dresses from the top names in designer fashion, allowing you to rent extravagant outfits that are typically only admired in clothing catalogs. Rentals on RentTheRunway typically last for four days and range from fifty to four hundred dollars. These outfits are shipped directly to your door, along with a prepaid envelope for returning them. To avoid the chance of your attire being a poor fit, a backup size is included free of cost.

Other popular websites for renting women's apparel include LendingLuxury.com and BagBorroworSteal.com, which rents handbags, purses, sunglasses, and jewelry by the month. These sites have gained a large following in recent years and are likely to continue to grow in popularity.

MensWearhouse.com is a good option if you are interested in renting men's apparel. On the website you simply pick out a tux and accessories from hundreds of options, print out the page where it's displayed, and bring it in to one of the company's nine hundred locations nationwide. Once you arrive at one of the stores, a formal wear consultant will help you make sure your outfit is an ideal fit.

In addition to Men's Warehouse, there may be a number of other stores that rent tuxedos in your local area. Depending on where you live, local rental services are likely to offer the most competitive rates.

HOME FURNISHING

Shop at Off-Price Retailers and Liquidators

Home furnishings often require a hands-on inspection before making a purchase. As a result, shopping online tends to be a poor choice. Thankfully, there are other good ways to save money on these items right in your neighborhood.

The popular off-price retail chain HomeGoods offers great deals on home furnishing. At their stores you can often find appealing bargains on furniture, kitchenware, rugs, lamps, bedding, bathware, seasonable merchandise, and wall décor. Like most other off-price retailers, HomeGoods sells top-of-the-line brand-name products for up to a 60 percent discount. A similar chain, Big Lots, may also be worth visiting. However, unlike HomeGoods, Big Lots does not offer premium brands and has not received consistent consumer reviews.

Liquidators are also good stores to visit for discounted mattresses, furniture, carpets, and home appliances. Similar to off-price retailers, liquidators feature brand-name merchandise at deep discounts. Most of the items they sell are bought directly from manufacturers and department stores. These items tend to be slightly outdated models, previously used floor displays, and inventory that has acquired minor marks or scratches. Typically liquidators knock 30 to 70 percent off the original price of their merchandise. Prices are often negotiable, so feel free to haggle when something catches your eye. You can find liquidators in your area by running a search engine query with the name of the city in which you live and the word "liquidator."

Consider Visiting Outlets

Most mattress and furniture outlets are owned and operated by department stores or showrooms. After observing the success that liquidators have had, these major players thought they, too, should get in on the action. Outlets have a nearly identical business model to liquidators, but they tend to have more inventory on hand.

Generally, cheaper prices can be found at liquidators, but it's worth seeing what outlets have to offer, especially if you are making a major purchase like a new mattress or sofa. When visiting these stores, test the waters and see how the sales representative responds to a little bargaining. You are likely to be surprised by how much money you can save simply by suggesting a lower price.

Check Craigslist When Applicable

Most consumers don't mind buying certain items, like wooden furniture, secondhand. In addition to saving money, you can also minimize time and frustration by getting preassembled fixtures. Although secondhand stores are an option, Craigslist tends to have cheaper prices on most of these items.

When buying secondhand furniture, make sure you thoroughly inspect each item you are considering. First and foremost, ensure it doesn't smell of smoke or pets. Additionally, don't just do a visual inspection of the top or front of the fixture; also examine its backside. Often you can better identify repairs or damage from this angle since nobody is concerned with a glue line showing there. Checking the item for sturdiness is also important. Give it a good shake, and if it has legs, give them a tug. Reviewing these elements will not only ensure you get furniture in good condition but will also give you a solid negotiating edge if a minor defect is detected.

Save Money at Department Stores and Showrooms

If liquidators, outlets, and secondhand items put a sour taste in your mouth, you should still be able to save money on home furnishings at department stores and showrooms. A simple way to do this is to buy discounted gift cards from the previously mentioned websites that specialize in this exchange. You should be able to find discounted gift cards for most chains that feature these items, including home improvement stores such as Home Depot and Lowe's.

For those who are more interested in savings than in quality, IKEA may be a good place to shop for furniture. Just keep in mind that most of the items sold there are designed to be assembled by consumers. If the thought of assembling your own furniture sounds like more of a hassle than the savings are worth, check out IKEA's as-is section. This department contains deeply discounted preassembled returns.

If you are not in a rush to get your furniture, you may also want to take advantage of IKEA's twice-a-year clearance sale. At these times, selected items are discounted up to 70 percent to clear out old inventory and make way for new arrivals. Usually these sales take place in the summer and winter at most IKEA locations.

ELECTRONICS

Visit a Product Review Website

Product-related research won't be required for all your electronic purchases, but in many cases it can be tremendously insightful. Taking a few minutes to read through a handful of reviews will help ensure you get the best bang for your buck, regardless of your budget. Among the many product review websites, ConsumerSearch.com and ConsumerReports.org stand in a class of their own.

ConsumerSearch.com is an ideal choice for the majority of consumers who buy a few electronics each year. Unlike ConsumerReports.org, this site is completely free to use. In addition, it puts a stronger focus on budget models than do similar sites.

ConsumerReports.org tends to be a better option for those who spend a significant amount of money on electronics each year. This website is owned and operated by the Consumers Union, an independent nonprofit organization that has existed since 1936. The Consumers Union does not accept outside advertising and employs hundreds of mystery shoppers and technical experts who buy and test evaluated products. Its testing and research center is the largest of its kind in the world.

The primary advantage to using ConsumerReports.org over ConsumerSearch.com is having a bigger pool of reviewed items from which to choose. Additionally, ConsumerReports .org updates its reviews more often. At present, a membership to ConsumerReports.org costs thirty dollars for an annual subscription or seven dollars for a monthly subscription. If nothing else, you might want to consider subscribing to the website for a month prior to making a major purchase.

Visiting a product review website may take fifteen minutes, but taking the time to do this is likely to be worth its weight in gold. If you're not sold on this concept, try it out in the near future. My guess is that after using this effortless tool just once you will be convinced of its insight and value.

Compare Prices on Notable Websites

After deciding which electronic model you want, I suggest comparing prices on a handful of websites. Amazon.com, eBay.com, Newegg.com, TigerDirect.com, and Rakuten.com (formerly Buy.com) are all good websites to visit. When you compare prices on these sites, be sure to review the refund policy of each seller. Sometimes it's worth paying a few extra dollars for extra peace of mind.

As opposed to visiting different websites directly, many consumers opt to use price comparison websites, such as PriceGrabber.com, Shopzilla.com, and NextTag.com, when they are shopping for electronics. Generally this is a bad idea because these aggregators often overlook premium deals owing to complicated online coding and old data feeds.

Consider Buying Refurbished Electronics

Refurbished electronics typically cost 20 to 50 percent less than new models. Most refurbs come with a one-year warranty and usually undergo stricter quality control measures than new machines. Although some of these items are returned and repaired after months of use, most refurbs are sent back to their manufacturers within 30 days of the date they were purchased. These items are usually returned by customers taking advantage of the 30-day money-back guarantee that most retail stores and websites offer. Many times, when consumers do this, there's absolutely nothing wrong with the item they purchased. In most cases customers either couldn't figure out how to operate the item or decided they wanted a different model instead.

Refurbs are guaranteed to work just as well as brand-new electronics but may contain minor cosmetic damage such as a small dent or scratch. If appearance is a concern, stick to buying new items. Otherwise, try to find refurbished models before paying significantly more money for nearly identical machines.

Pass on Extended Warranties

Extended warranties have become a great tool for retail stores and e-commerce sites to increase their revenue. Surprisingly, it's estimated that Best Buy and similar chains make close to 50 percent of their profits from these last-minute purchases. Truth be told, the odds are heavily stacked against extended warranties ever paying off. Ninety-five percent of electronics work just fine during their first four years of life. Because electronics depreciate in value after a year or two, you can usually replace a broken item with the same refurnished model for a fraction of its cost. Even when it comes to expensive electronics, such as computers, you are typically better off skipping this unnecessary expense.

What you can do for extra peace of mind, is use a major credit card to buy electronics, which in most cases will extend original manufacturer warranties by one year. American Express, Discover, Visa, and MasterCard all offer extended warranty protection as a perk on most of their credit cards. Among these four, American Express has the most lenient policy, which also extends coverage to refurbished electronics.

Buy Discounted Accessories and Cables

If you are interested in top-of-the-line accessories, it pays to visit ConsumerSearch.com or ConsumerReports.org to compare different models. However, for most electronic accessories, lesser-known brands are comparable to brand-name options and tend to be substantially cheaper. An easy way to identify quality products is to look over consumer reviews on Amazon.com. Literally hundreds of thousands of reviews have been submitted on Amazon for an endless number of products. Quickly scanning over these reviews can help you find great bargains.

Likewise, the same cables that cost you an arm and a leg at Radio Shack can be found on Amazon and eBay for up to an 80 percent discount. Though they may not bear a Radio Shack logo or look quite as pretty, they will serve the same purpose as their fancy counterparts.

If you can afford it, buying digital cables is a sensible investment, as they do produce a better connection than ordinary cables. However, as long as generic cables are the same type and gauge as brand-name options, they will produce the exact same picture and sound. Brand-name cables may be made of better materials and are likely to be more durable, but that will not translate to any audio or visual difference. Considering that generic cables cost up to 80 percent less than brand-name options, it makes very little sense to spend so much more money for something that will not produce any tangible results.

Save Money on Printer Ink and Batteries

Printer ink is one of the most expensive liquids on earth, costing thousands of dollars per gallon. Although you could be frugal with your ink and print only on an as-needed basis, a better option is to find ways to buy it at a fraction of its cost.

Buying generic cartridges online is a good way to reduce the cost of ink and toner by at least 50 percent. Most consumers find generic ink and toner to work just fine for basic printing needs. If there's something that you need printed with flawless detail, you can always have it done at a retail store that offers printing services.

Another equally inexpensive option is to take your ink or toner cartridges to a retail store to be refilled. Costco and Walgreens are among the nationwide chains that refill ink and toner cartridges at many locations.

For more ambitious consumers, ink and toner refill kits are commonly sold online and at office supply stores. Refill kits are the cheapest option available, but be forewarned: refilling your ink can be a very messy job. It's highly recommended that you cover your work area with newspapers and use disposable gloves, at least the first couple of times you attempt the task.

Perhaps the easiest way to save money on printer ink is to ensure that you get the full life out of each cartridge. When your computer gives you a warning that your printer ink or toner is low, don't just replace it; take your cartridge out and give it a thorough shake. This will usually result in an extra hundred pages of use.

Saving money on batteries is another easy feat that can be accomplished by making a one-time investment in rechargeable batteries. Unlike a few years ago, you can now get nickel metal hydride (NiMH) rechargeable batteries that come precharged and maintain 90 percent of their power, even after sitting idle for six months. Like the last generation of rechargeable batteries, they can be reused hundreds of times. The cost for a charger with four AA or AAA NiMH batteries starts at around fifteen dollars. Considering how inexpensive this is, it's a wonder why shoppers would repeatedly purchase single-use alkaline batteries over and over again.

HOW MUCH MONEY CAN YOU SAVE ON CLOTHING AND HOUSEHOLD ITEMS?

Saving method	Average savings
Buying clothing at off-price retailers	40% compared to standard retail pricing
Buying home furnishing at liquidators	40% compared to standard retail pricing
Buying refurbished electronics	30% compared to new products
Using NiMH rechargeable batteries	100% more cost-effective than using alkaline batteries

CHAPTER SEVEN

AUTOMOTIVE EXPENSES

Most Americans will spend over half a million dollars on vehicle-related expenses in their lifetimes. Although this figure is shocking, few people would sacrifice their vehicles or compromise its reliability to save a few dollars. Fortunately, there are other ways to save money on automotive expenses.

ROUTINE MAINTENANCE

Save Money on Oil Changes and Tune-Ups

Getting routine oil changes and tune-ups is one of the best ways to avoid monstrous expenses down the line. A poorly tuned car is not only likely to shorten the life of expensive engine components but may also exhibit poor gas mileage as a symptom of neglect. However, although it's important to keep up on preventative maintenance, you don't want to get oil changes and tune-ups more often than is necessary. Mechanics and oil companies are quick to recommend getting an oil change every three thousand miles, but in reality they are the ones benefiting most from this timetable. Although decades ago, this suggestion was valid, cars are now designed for less frequent oil changes. If you have a car that was built within the last twenty years, you shouldn't need to change its oil before five thousand miles.

Similarly, most mechanics suggest getting intense and expensive tune-ups more often than they are truly needed. To avoid wasting money on these expenses, it's a good idea to review and follow the schedules for preventative maintenance in your vehicle's owner's manual. These instructions will almost always be less stringent than your mechanic's recommendations and are guaranteed to meet your vehicle's unique and specific needs.

Do the Easy Stuff Yourself

Doing a few easy tasks yourself is another good way to save money on maintenance expenses. For example, just about anyone can change burned-out headlights and replace broken windshield wiper blades. If you are not sure how to do these tasks, visit the website DoItYourself.com for simple, step-by-step instructions.

You can also save money by inspecting your vehicle's air

filter every few months and replacing it as needed. According to the EPA, a dirty air filter can reduce your fuel efficiency by up to 10 percent as a result of poor airflow. Air filters usually cost about ten dollars and typically take less than ten minutes to replace.

To inspect your car's air filter, consult your vehicle's owner's manual to see exactly where it's located. After taking it out, hold it up to natural sunlight. It you have trouble seeing through it, it's time to change it. The life span of your filter depends on where you live and how dusty and dirty the roads on which you travel are. Inspecting the air filter every few months is the best way to ensure that it's still in good shape.

When your vehicle needs a new air filter, you can either order one online or pick one up at an auto shop according to your vehicle's make and model. By doing this simple task yourself, you should save about fifty dollars. If you would rather not get your hands dirty, make sure you have your car's air filter inspected every time the vehicle gets an oil change.

REPAIRS

Self-Diagnose Your Automobile

In the past, it was very easy for mechanics to take advantage of our automotive ignorance, but today this is no longer the case. Now, when something is wrong with your vehicle, you should be able to diagnose the problem and acquire an accurate repair estimate with minimal effort.

If your vehicle was built after 1996, it will have a standard EPA-mandated OBD II system (On-Board Diagnostics, version II). OBD II systems collect information from all the major mechanical components in your automobile and should immediately indicate when something is wrong by turning on the "check engine" light. When your check engine light comes on, the easiest way to find out exactly what is wrong with your vehicle is to use an automotive diagnostic scanner. Any and every auto shop should have one of these handy. Most shops will either let you use its scanner free of charge or will rent it to you for a small fee.

If your vehicle was built before 1996 and doesn't contain an OBD II system, it may be challenging to find an auto shop with a compatible scanner. Even if you do manage to locate one, most shops will charge you a hefty fee to use it. In such cases it's advisable to get the problem checked by a mechanic who is familiar with your vehicle's make and model.

After identifying what is wrong with your automobile, pay a visit to RepairPal.com and click on its "Estimator" tab. After entering the repair or service you need, RepairPal will provide you with an estimate based on the part of the country in which you live. In addition, RepairPal will automatically separate the cost of parts and labor for those who want to buy their auto parts independently. Taking a few minutes to acquire this information will help you anticipate what kinds of expenses are on the horizon and should prevent dishonest mechanics from swindling you out of cash.

Find a Good Mechanic

If you don't currently have a mechanic who you have used in the past and trust, you should be able to find one with ease. To simplify your search, focus on independently owned auto shops. Independently owned shops are almost always cheaper than dealerships and tend to do much better work than chains. Because the quality and rates at these shops can vary, it's a good idea to seek out referrals from family, friends, and colleagues. As just about everyone owns a vehicle, making a few phone calls should lead to at least two or three recommendations.

Instead of jumping on one of these referrals, set these phone numbers aside and visit a consumer review website for further recommendations. Yelp.com is a great website to use for this purpose. Yelp has more reviews for auto shops than any other consumer review site and has a reliable filter that catches and weeds out the majority of malicious and owner-manipulated comments.

Between personal recommendations and well-reviewed shops, you should have a decent list of options. To help confirm that the mechanics on your list are trustworthy, visit the Better Business Bureau's website at BBB.org. After entering your zip code and clicking on the "Check Out a Business" tab, you will be able to see if any of these shops have consumer complaints on file. This should take only a minute or two and may help weed out a few bad seeds.

At this point you should be ready to compare baseline estimates from the auto shops on your list. While making these inquiries, you may also want to ask about buying auto parts independently. Even though buying your own auto parts will void your service warranty, it will often save you hundreds of dollars. If this concept is new to you, don't worry—this task is not as challenging as it sounds. Thanks to e-commerce sites, auto parts are far more accessible than they were in the past. As a result, many consumers are making this request, and most independently owned shops have no objection.

Buy Quality Auto Parts

Auto parts fall into two categories: original equipment manufacturer (OEM) parts and aftermarket parts. OEM parts are identical to the parts that came with your vehicle, whereas aftermarket parts are made by different manufacturers. OEM parts are generally more expensive, but they also tend to be more reliable. That being said, at times aftermarket parts can be superior. For example, top-of-the-line aftermarket spark plugs and brake pads tend to be better than their OEM counterparts.

Before deciding whether to buy aftermarket parts, spend a few minutes doing a little bit of research. The best place to get auto part guidance is on online forums related to your vehicle. You can locate these forums by running a query with any search engine containing the make and model of your vehicle plus the word "forum." Once you have located a relevant forum, conduct queries with the names of the replacement parts you need. This process should lead to a number of recommendations from other drivers who had to get the same repair done in the past.

After deciding which parts you want to buy, order them from a nearby auto parts store or e-commerce site, such as Motors.eBay.com, JCWhitney.com, or AutoPartsWarehouse.com. When expensive parts are needed, you may want to consider buying them secondhand, especially if they are nonmechanical. Again, online forums can help you with this decision. Although buying secondhand parts has obvious drawbacks, the savings often outweigh the disadvantages. Typically, used auto parts cost about 70 percent less than new components, providing a unique opportunity to save money.

Car-Part.com is a great website for tracking down any secondhand part you desire. Unlike other e-commerce sites mentioned, Car-Part.com does not sell parts directly to consumers. Instead, it will provide you with contact information for independent sellers and junk yards in your area that have the parts you require. Next to the contact information for each seller will be a detailed description of the part's condition and the seller's asking price. If any parts that you need are not available, wait a few days and check the site again.

Thousands of sellers are connected with Car-Part.com, and inventories are updated daily.

Motors.eBay.com is another good website from which to buy secondhand parts, particularly when lightweight components are needed. Similarly to Car-Part.com, eBay's inventory should include any automotive part you require.

GAS

Buy Inexpensive Gas

Most thrifty consumers have no problem driving a little out of their way to fill up on an inexpensive tank of gas. To help consumers locate reasonably priced fuel, a number of websites have sprung up, including the tremendously popular site GasBuddy.com. GasBuddy has a network of loyal followers who constantly post appealing gas prices as they see them. Thanks to these posts, you are likely to find nearby gas stations with reasonably priced fuel, regardless of where you live in the country.

Using GasBuddy sounds great in theory, but in reality this strategy will rarely save you money. The only time it's sensible to make a point of filling up with an inexpensive tank of gas is when doing so does not require any kind of a commute. If you are a Costco member, it makes sense to buy gas when you are already there shopping, because Costco tends to have great rates. In addition, Arco is a good place to get reasonably priced gas if you have one in your neighborhood. Although it's true that Arco does not have the fancy additives that Chevron and Shell claim to use, it's worth noting that these additives have not been proven to do anything for the longevity of your engine or to result in better gas mileage. In fact, after testing over one hundred additives, the EPA concluded that most gas additive claims were nothing more than empty marketing pitches and lies.

There are also many myths about premium gasoline. The most common claim is that it prolongs the life of engines and allows vehicles to run better, but there's no research to support this statement. On the contrary, leading scientists, engineers, and the federal government all agree that buying premium gas is downright wasteful. Even if your automobile is one of the few vehicles for which the owner's manual recommends premium gas, using it will not help the life of engine components or minimize the need for routine maintenance. In such cases, the only detectable difference between premium and regular gas is a slight increase in horsepower. While this increased horsepower may be "detectable," it's next to unnoticeable.

Reduce Your Gas Consumption

The best way to reduce your gas consumption is to drive as smoothly and steadily as you can. Most drivers can maintain a fairly unaltered speed in routine traffic but tend to let their frustrations get the best of them during rush hour. With the right amount of restraint, even in extremely heavy traffic, it's relatively easy to maintain a steady speed without overusing your brake pedal. The key to this practice is keeping a comfortable distance from the car in front of you and being mindful of the line of cars ahead. Doing this will enable you to anticipate slowdowns and should improve your fuel economy by an average of 20 percent.

Likewise, maintaining a steady speed on highways and freeways can help your gas mileage. According to the U.S. government, each five miles you drive over sixty miles per hour increases your fuel consumption by 10 percent. Using cruise control can help with this by avoiding unconscious accelerations.

Other noteworthy suggestions to reduce gas consumption include not sitting idle for more than thirty seconds at a stretch, ensuring your tires are properly inflated by checking your tire pressure once each month, and keeping the weight down in your trunk. These secondary suggestions should improve your fuel economy up to 5 percent.

PARKING

If you live in a major city, parking can be a hefty expense. Often in downtown districts, daily parking rates can vary by as much as ten dollars an hour within a two-block radius. Likewise, when it comes to monthly parking rates, walking an extra two minutes can sometimes save you twenty dollars a month. Thankfully, finding cheap parking has never been easier.

Rather than driving around in circles looking for reasonable parking, you can visit an extremely helpful website that has done this work for you. BestParking.com provides a free parking search engine that directs drivers to the cheapest paid parking available. Consumers can search for inexpensive parking by neighborhood, address, cross street, or landmark. While BestParking does not cover every city in the United States, its territory does include over eighty major cities in North America and almost every major airport in the country.

If you live in a city that BestParking does not cover, visit a search engine and conduct a query inquiring where cheap parking can be found near the address, venue, or attraction you are visiting. Taking the time to do this two-minute exercise should save you money, time, and unnecessary frustration.

BUYING AN AUTOMOBILE

Consider Buying a Used Vehicle

Buying a used vehicle is one of the smartest financial decisions you can make. New cars depreciate in value an average of 25 percent in the first year. Essentially, that means you are paying a quarter of the car's overall cost for one year of use. Even if you can afford a new vehicle, think about what kind of used car you could get with the same amount of money. If warranties and certifications are a concern, you can now buy used cars with both of these, which should give you the same peace of mind you have when you turn the key in a new vehicle for the first time.

When you buy a used car, you will also save money on insurance costs and can frequently find much bigger bargains than at a new car lot. Likewise, used cars are much more reliable than they ever were before. Thanks to Carfax.com, you can view a complete history of the vehicle you are considering on an easy-to-read report, which will inform you of the vehicle's owner history, accident history, state admission inspection results, and other useful information.

If you're one of those people who just loves the way a new car smells, keep in mind that the scent you relish is nothing more than toxic fumes emitting from plastic, glue, and paint. In fact, a two-year study conducted in Australia found several health problems associated with these fumes, shedding light on the many new car drivers who complain about headaches, sore throats, drowsiness, and nausea.

Buy a Fuel-Efficient Automobile

Buying a fuel-efficient automobile is something to consider when you are selecting your next vehicle. In most cases, smaller vehicles tend to get better gas mileage than larger ones. As a result, it would be wise to buy the smallest automobile for your needs.

A good website to help you compare the fuel consumption of different vehicles is FuelEconomy.gov. Once you log onto the site, select the "Find a Car" tab in the upper lefthand corner and enter the year, make, and model of each vehicle you are considering. After running your query, you will be able to view the city, highway, and combined fuel consumption rates for all of your entries. If you are unsure how much this will impact your finances, use the miles-per-gallon calculator on their website. Going through this exercise should give you a good idea of which cars on your short list will add to or reduce your monthly expenses.

Buy a Reliable Automobile

When conducting vehicle-related research, it's always best to use multiple sources. Two of the best websites to consult are ConsumerReports.org and Edmunds.com. Consumer-Reports.org charges a small monthly fee, but based on the importance of this investment, you shouldn't think twice about paying it for a month or two.

As previously mentioned, you should also use Carfax .com to view a complete history of any used vehicle you are seriously considering. Instead of purchasing a single report for forty dollars, consider purchasing unlimited reports for fifty-five dollars, in case the first car you're eyeing doesn't check out. AutoCheck.com also offers similar data for slightly more reasonable fees.

Getting a prepurchase inspection (PPI) conducted is also a must before buying any used vehicle. If you have a mechanic you like and trust, use him or her for this task. Otherwise, try using the service department of a dealership or a repair shop specializing in the make and model of the vehicle you are considering. A PPI should cost about one hundred dollars, so it's wise to have this done only with an automobile you are ready to buy. Although it's easy to talk yourself out of this investment, don't do it, as it could end up saving you thousands of dollars down the line.

Which vehicle you buy next will be one of the most important financial decisions you are likely to make. Take your time with it, and do plenty of research to ensure that your next automobile serves your needs and long-term saving goals.

HOW MUCH MONEY CAN YOU SAVE ON AUTOMOTIVE EXPENSES?

Saving method	Average savings
Using your owner's manual for maintenance timelines	30% compared to standard suggestions
Buying auto parts independently	40% compared to standard repair shop pricing
Anticipating slowdowns and moderately accelerating while driving	15% of your fuel consumption
Maintaining a steady speed on highways, without exceeding 60 mph	10% of your fuel consumption

CHAPTER EIGHT

ADDITIONAL SHOPPING STRATEGIES

In addition to the many saving methods discussed in previous chapters, a few more strategies can be used when you're shopping online for products or services. Taking a few moments to utilize these suggestions should put extra money in your pocket with minimal effort.

AUCTION SNIPING

Most thrifty consumers shop on eBay.com throughout the year. eBay is a great website from which to buy just about anything. Typically, eBay shoppers bid on items that catch their eye or use eBay's "Buy It Now" and "Best Offer" features. A fourth option that savvy buyers utilize is *sniping,* an eBay bidding strategy that involves placing a bid in the final seconds of an auction.

Sniping has been proven to result in more winning bids and lower purchase prices than other auction strategies. Sniping not only avoids bidding wars but also limits *bid chasing,* which is when the presence of your bid encourages others to place bids on the same item. Consumers frequently inspect the bidding history on auctions as a way of determining the true value of a product. They are more likely to place a bid when there are multiple bids on an item, a trend which results in higher purchase prices.

Although some consumers object to sniping and claim it to be unfair, it's perfectly legal. eBay recently addressed this debate and issued a written statement in the website article "Getting Outbid." According to eBay, "sniping is part of the eBay experience and all bids placed before a listing ends are valid." Sniping can be done manually, with computer software, or by using an online sniping service. Manual sniping is the poorest option of the three, as it requires that you be in front of your computer in the final minutes before bidding ends. Using sniping software is a better option, though your computer needs to be turned on for your bid to be placed, which isn't always convenient or good for your motherboard.

That leaves us with online services, which offer the most convenient sniping method available. Websites that offer this service place your bid for you whether your computer is on or off, and whether you are at work or asleep in your bed. Online sniping services all operate more or less the same way. After finding an item that you want to buy, you then enter its eBay item number, along with the maximum amount you want to bid on their website. Once this is done, the sniping service will place your bid three or four seconds before the auction ends. When the auction is over, you will be notified via e-mail if you won or lost. If you did win, you will be responsible for a small service fee of around 1 percent of the auction price.

When you use an online sniping service, you must share your eBay ID and password with them. As a result, it's extremely important to use a trustworthy website. At present, eSnipe.com is the most secure and reliable website of this type, placing over ten thousand bids a day. Thanks to its high-level data encryption, eSnipe has been recommended by numerous organizations, including the *New York Times*, which described eSnipe as "the industry standard."

ONLINE COUPON CODES

Although many thrifty shoppers take advantage of paper coupons, very few consumers regularly use online coupon codes. Online coupon codes are often available for e-commerce sites and can be located in less than a minute. Typically, coupon codes offer free shipping or five to ten dollars off your order.

When you are shopping online, keep a keen eye out for

a small box that says "coupon code" or "promotional code" during the checkout process. If you see such a box, take a moment to search for a coupon code. The easiest way to do this is to open up another window with your favorite search engine and conduct a query with the retailer's name followed by "coupon code." This query will usually lead you to a few-money saving codes from which to choose.

After exploring these discounts, plug the best one you can find into the online order form and click on the "Apply Now" tab. If the coupon code has expired, the website will bring up a message saying so, but if it's valid, it will deduct the correct amount from your order. If the first code you try doesn't work, try a handful more. After all, it takes just a few minutes to try five or six codes, and there's a fairly good chance at least one will be valid.

Instead of using a search engine, you could use a coupon code aggregator such as RetailMeNot.com, ShopGala.com, or CouponCabin.com. However, search engines generally pull data from all these sites, giving you access to a bigger playing field.

ONLINE REBATES

Online rebates may not be as lucrative as coupon codes, but getting them is just as easy. Most rebates available online are offered through rebate portals. Rebate portals are independent websites that pay you between 1 and 10 percent of your total purchase price from popular e-commerce sites. Websites that have offered discounts through rebate portals include eBay.com, WalMart.com, TigerDirect.com, JCPenney.com, DrugStore.com, and Target.com.

Rebate portals can afford to pay you rebates because online retailers pay them a commission for directing traffic to their websites. In return, they share part of this money with you. Depending on the portal, your rebate will be paid in cash, with airline miles, or with a donation to a collage savings plan or charity. Personally, I suggest using cash-back portals so you have the freedom to spend your rebates as you wish.

Cash-back rebate portals will typically pay you through a PayPal account or by sending you a check in the mail. These payments are usually disbursed every three months or on request, once you have at least five or ten dollars in your account. It's a good idea to use just one or two rebate portals so you frequently achieve the minimum cash-back requirements. Currently your two best options are Ebates .com and MrRebate.com. Both websites feature hundreds of e-commerce sites and are trustworthy and user-friendly.

Instead of visiting Ebates.com and MrRebate.com directly, run a search engine query with the name of the online retailer you are shopping with, followed by "Ebates," then "MrRebate." If a rebate is available through either of these websites, your search results will provide a direct link to the portal. You can run this two-second query right after you search for coupon codes.

DEAL-HUNTING WEBSITES

Deal-hunting websites have truly revolutionized bargain shopping. These online bazaars list a variety of deals from numerous websites and retail stores. In most cases, the deals they feature are valid only for a few days or while supplies last. As a result, try to take advantage of appealing offers as you see them.

It's a good idea to visit deal-hunting websites when you are looking for a specific item but are open to buying different brands and models. They are also nice outlets for gift shopping. Just be careful not to be lured into buying an item you don't need or want just because you can get it for a bargain.

Some of the better deal-hunting websites to visit are DealNews.com, SlickDeals.net, BradsDeals.com, BensBargains.net, and TechBargains.com. DealNews, SlickDeals, and TechBargains are good websites to shop for electronics. BradsDeals and BensBargains tend to be better options for random products. Thankfully, most deal-hunting sites contain user ratings next to each deal. Deals with higher ratings are usually valid and tend to offer the deepest discounts. Zoom in on these offers and ignore the deals with low ratings, as they are likely to be outdated or subpar.

DAILY DEAL WEBSITES

In the past few years, a new flock of e-commerce sites have emerged that offer one or more items for sale for a period of 24 to 36 hours. These sites usually feature electronics, but at times they offer a range of other interesting things. Typically these products are sold at a 30 to 70 percent discount, providing good opportunities to pick up desired items or future gifts for stunning bargains. Because most daily deal websites have only a small inventory of each item, products often sell out a few hours after a sale begins. Likewise, at the end of the day, featured items are no longer offered or available, so if you see an appealing deal, it's a good idea to jump on it in a timely fashion. Woot.com, DailySteals.com, 1Sale.com, and Yugster.com are the most popular websites of this nature.

GROUP BUYING WEBSITES

Group buying websites use the power of collective bargaining to reduce prices with local and national business. Most of the deals featured on these websites are for restaurants, events, activities, spas, and home and auto services. In addition, some group buying sites also have superb deals for one-night or two-night getaways in luxury hotels and resorts. Like daily deal sites, most of these offers are available in limited quantities and for a short period of time.

Groupon.com and LivingSocial.com are the most popular

group buying websites. Both sites have millions of subscribers and currently offer deals in over 150 markets in North America. GoldStar.com, SweetJack.com, and GiltCity.com are similar websites based on this successful business model.

Even Amazon and Google have recently tried their hand at group buying websites. Currently they only cover limited cities in the United States but often have appealing offers. Visit Local.Amazon.com and Google.com/offers to check out their current deals.

If you find yourself participating in a number of group deals throughout the year, you may want to create an account with Yipit.com. Yipit is a group buying aggregator that recommends local deals to you based on your account preferences. You can receive Yipit's recommendations in a personalized e-mail or by logging on to the website.

HOW MUCH MONEY CAN YOU SAVE WITH THESE SHOPPING STRATEGIES?

Saving method	Average savings
Sniping auctions on eBay	5% of your total purchase price
Applying online coupon codes when applicable	5% of your total purchase price
Applying online rebates when applicable	5% of your total purchase price
Using deal-hunting websites to find desired products	50% compared to standard retail pricing
Participating in group buying deals	50% compared to standard rates

CHAPTER NINE

RESTAURANTS AND ENTERTAINMENT

There are many penny-pinching strategies to save money on entertainment. Some of the most common suggestions include eating out for lunch instead of dinner, going to the movies during the afternoon to take advantage of matinee prices, and seeking out free concerts and performances to avoid spending money on live entertainment. I don't know about you, but I much prefer having a nice romantic dinner with my wife after a hard day of work, as opposed to meeting her for a quick meal during my lunch break. Likewise, going to a movie theater during the afternoon just doesn't feel the same as ending the day with a good movie. And I certainly have no interest in seeing a subpar band perform. I would be much happier listening to good album at home.

Fortunately, by using a few strategies, you can save money

on the type of entertainment you currently enjoy. In fact, if you follow the saving methods summarized in this chapter, you will likely find yourself seeing and doing more things than ever before.

RESTAURANTS

Buy an Entertainment Book

The Entertainment Book is a region-specific coupon book that is available for over one hundred cities in the United States. Each edition features an outstanding variety of coupons for just about every type of cuisine imaginable. Typically, these coupons offer two entrées for the price of one or a similar discount. New editions of the Entertainment Book come out every September, and most coupons in the book are valid until November of the following year. Naturally, it pays to get your book as close to its publication date as you can, but if you happen to be on the market for one later in the year, don't hesitate to buy a copy. As the year progresses, the price of each edition will go down steadily in cost to compensate for lost savings opportunities.

In addition to coupons for restaurants, the Entertainment Book is also filled with coupons for retail stores, travel websites, car rental agencies, and other forms of entertainment and services. If you find yourself using a number of these coupons, you should think about buying two or three copies of each edition. Just keep in mind that it may be poorly perceived to use the same coupon more than once at independently owned restaurants.

When your Entertainment Book first arrives, it's helpful to spend some time looking through it. As you flip through your book, note down all the offers that appeal to you. Record the name of the business, the value of the coupon, and its page number. Once you have completed your list, attach it to the inside cover of the coupon book. Doing so may sound like a pointless activity, but remember that out of sight often equals out of mind. Completing this easy exercise will remind you of the many coupons that you want to use before the year is over.

You can naturally get more miles out of the Entertainment Book if you live with a partner or a child. However, even if you live alone, buying a book is bound to pay off, particularly if you get together with friends for dinner now and then. In fact, using only two or three coupons will typically cover the cost of each edition. You can purchase the latest editions of the Entertainment Book at Entertainment.com.

Log on to Restaurant.com

Restaurant.com is a nice supplementary source for restaurant discounts. This helpful website allows you to buy discounted, print-at-home dining certificates for a diverse range of restaurants in your local community. The dining certificates sold on Restaurant.com do not expire, and you are welcome to use one certificate per month for each restaurant you select. With a little luck, this website will feature a number of restaurants that you routinely visit and enjoy. Because the restaurants promoted on the site frequently change, when you find an appealing certificate, you may want to buy more than one.

All the dining certificates featured on Restaurant.com carry a stipulation requiring you to spend a certain amount of money on your meal before your certificate can be redeemed. The most common certificates sold on this site require a minimum purchase of thirty-five dollars, have a twenty-five dollar value, and cost ten dollars. There are also four dollar certificates with a ten dollar value that require a minimum purchase of fifteen dollars. Although these stipulations may be a nuisance, they are not hard to meet even if you are dining with just one other person. Order two main courses, drinks, and an appetizer or dessert, and you will easily reach the minimum requirements for a twenty-five dollar certificate. If you are not interested in appetizers or dessert, buy the ten dollar dining certificates and save money on a simple one-course meal.

While saving five to fifteen dollars on a nice meal out isn't bad, you can multiply your savings dramatically by taking one additional step. Currently numerous one hundred dollar gift cards for Restaurant.com are being sold on eBay around the clock. These gift cards can be used to purchase four twenty-five dollar certificates, or any other combination of certificates, and do not need to be used all at once. The going rate for a one hundred dollar gift card is currently around five dollars. By making this purchase, you will significantly increase your savings, allowing you to buy $25 dining certificates for just $1.25.

To capitalize on this opportunity, log in to your eBay account and conduct a general search for Restaurant.com. After running your query, you are likely to find hundreds of gift cards being sold at a fraction of their value. Over the past few years, there has been an endless supply of these gift cards available, but who knows how long this will last. Capitalizing on money-saving suggestions as you become aware of them is the best way to avoid missing out on good deals.

MOVIES

Buy Discounted Movie Tickets

Who doesn't love to go to the movies? From childhood this has been a favorite form of entertainment for most of us. Unfortunately, these days, most movie theaters charge about ten dollars for a ticket and another ten dollars for popcorn and soda. Sure, you could catch a matinee or see a film at one of the three-dollar theaters that show movies months after they come out, but let's face it, seeing a movie long after its release date just isn't the same. Thankfully, there are a couple of affordable ways to see movies in your favorite theaters at any time of the day.

Using the movie theater coupons in the Entertainment Book is the simplest way to save money on tickets. Most editions of the Entertainment Book contain coupons for nationwide cinema chains such as Regal and AMC. If it's not convenient to go to the cinemas featured in the Entertainment Book, consider buying movie passes. These passes are available for most cinema chains in the country and do not carry expiration dates. They can be purchased from a variety of organizations, including AAA, GEICO, Costco, and Sam's Club.

Using Entertainment Book coupons or movie passes should reduce the cost of your tickets by about 30 percent. Although this may not sound like a lot of money, it essentially gets you a matinee-priced ticket whenever you desire.

Get Your Snacks on the Way to the Theater

Most movie theaters make an 85 percent profit on the majority of items sold at concession stands. Although it's true that cinemas discourage outside food being brought in, there's nothing to prevent you from putting a snack or a bag of candy in your purse or pocket. Bringing your own snacks not only saves you money but also allows you the opportunity to opt for healthier choices. If going to the movies just isn't the same without a large bucket of buttered popcorn, then go for it.

Just be aware that in that tub is the same amount of calories and fat as a pound of baby back ribs topped off with a scoop of Häagen-Dazs ice cream.

CONCERTS, SPORTING EVENTS, AND LIVE THEATER

Look for Discounted Tickets Online

Getting discounted tickets is fairly easy for events that are not likely to sell out. The ideal time to look for such tickets is two weeks before the event. At this time, nervous ticket brokers become extra eager to sell off their unsold tickets, while a few consumers are compelled to unload their tickets owing to unexpected engagements or illness. In all these cases, ticket sellers are less concerned with making a profit than with minimizing their losses. This presents a great opportunity to get tickets for up to 80 percent below their face value.

eBay is a good place to start your hunt for discounted tickets. Because eBay has so many sellers, the competition often drives prices lower than other websites. In addition, because many sellers on eBay auction off their tickets, you can often get deals you won't find elsewhere.

StubHub.com, TicketsNow.com, TicketCity.com, RazorGator.com, and EmpireTickets.com are good secondary websites to explore when you can't find a desirable price on eBay. All these sites offer a 100 percent money-back guarantee, so you need not worry about getting fraudulent tickets. However, because most of them charge service fees, lower prices can usually be found on eBay.

If you prefer, you can always use a ticket aggregator, such as SeatGeek.com, instead of visiting each site individually. Just be cautious before doing business with websites other than the ones listed previously, as many e-commerce sites sell tickets these days, and not all of them provide security and protection.

Another option for finding discounted tickets is searching through the classified ads on Craigslist.com. Craigslist often has the cheapest ticket prices on the web but lacks the security of the other options discussed. Sellers who list tickets on Craigslist will almost always sell them below face value, especially if the event is less than a week away. Because most sellers on Craigslist reside in your local area, you also have the advantage of buying your tickets right up to the day of the show. Just keep in mind that buyers who are sold bogus tickets through Craigslist have no way to collect a refund. As a result, caution and sound judgment are required before making a purchase.

Take Advantage of Discount Ticket Booths

Discount ticket booths can be found in many cities across the country. Tickets available at these booths tend to be related to the performing arts, including plays, ballets, operas, and other live performances. Generally you can only buy tickets at discount booths in person and on the day of the show, but you can usually get an idea of the tickets they are selling by visiting their websites.

In most cases, discount ticket booths sell tickets for events that have been showing for some time. It's worth seeing what they have to offer if you want to see a performance of this nature or if you just want an evening out and are open to seeing a few different shows. You can expect to save up to 50 percent on your tickets when you take advantage of this service.

Currently discount ticket booths can be found in New York, Las Vegas, Chicago, San Francisco, Boston, San Diego, and Washington, DC, as well as other major cities. To find out if there's a booth near you, use a search engine to conduct a query with the city in which you live, followed by "discount ticket booth." The list of discount ticket booths is ever expanding, so if there isn't one in your local area today, there may be one in the near future.

Plan Ahead for Popular Events

When it comes to popular events that are likely to sell out, buying tickets in advance is the best way to get the most for your money. For years ticket brokers have used insider tricks and secrets to snag the most desirable tickets to sell them for outrageous profits. By taking advantage of the same methods, it's quite easy to get great seats at even the most sought-after events.

To begin this process, it's important to understand how ticket presales work. First and foremost, just about any popular event will have a ticket presale. Participating in presales gives you an exclusive opportunity to buy tickets before the general public. The tickets available during this time are not necessarily better than the tickets sold during the general public sale. However, because you will be competing to buy tickets with fewer fans, you are likely to end up with better seats.

To participate in presales, you'll need a password. The best place to get a hold of presale passwords and to find out when presales begin is through official fan clubs and newsletters related to the event. If you have a few favorite sports teams, musical artists, bands, or venues, it's not a bad idea to sign up for these in advance. That being said, if there's an event coming up that you want to see but don't have a presale password for, you should be able to find it online without too much trouble. At times you may be able to find passwords for free on different websites and blogs. More often than not, however, you will have to spend a few dollars to access this information. When this is the case, pay a visit to PresalePasswordInfo.com. This website tends to have the largest selection of active presale passwords available, and thankfully, before paying a dime, you will know if it has the password you require. Currently PresalePasswordInfo.com charges a flat fee of ten dollars for an annual membership, making this a small investment that is bound to pay off throughout the year.

After acquiring a password, it's crucial that you buy your tickets as soon as the sale begins. Keep in mind that this does not require any more effort or time than buying tickets a week down the line. If you happen to be working when a presale starts, take a quick ten-minute break right before presales begin. Purchasing great tickets shouldn't take more than a few minutes, but, as with many things, timing is everything. Trying to buy tickets even five minutes after a sale has started will often be a lost cause.

Assuming Ticketmaster is the merchant for the event, go to the Ticketmaster website five minutes prior to the sale. Make sure you are logged in to your Ticketmaster account and on the event page a few minutes before things get started. Then, open up a new window and visit Time.gov so you can ensure you are viewing an accurate clock with the seconds displayed. Once thirty seconds are left before the tickets go on sale, close this and any other open windows to ensure that your Internet connection is at top speed. Then, immediately return to Ticketmaster's event page and press the refresh button on your browser. Continue to refresh the screen every five seconds until the newly loaded ticket ordering page comes up. Don't hit the refresh button more often than this, as it could cause Ticketmaster to lock you out and make you log in to its website all over again.

After refreshing the screen a handful of times, you will likely get through to the ticket ordering page. At this time, select the pricing section and the number of tickets you desire as quickly as possible. Once this is completed, you will have access to great tickets that won't be available a few moments later.

If there isn't going to be a presale for an event that you want to see, you can use this same method to buy tickets during the general public sale. Even if the event isn't outrageously popular, using this strategy will get the best seats possible in the price range you desire.

OTHER FORMS OF ENTERTAINMENT

Make the Most of Your Entertainment Book

Besides having coupons for restaurants and movies, the Entertainment Book is loaded with coupons for other forms of entertainment. Depending on where you live, it may include coupons for museums, fairs, bowling alleys, amusement parks, water parks, local cruises, and a host of other outings. Utilizing such coupons is a good way to save money and experience the different types of entertainment your local area has to offer.

In addition, there may be other coupon books available for your city. If you see a coupon book of this type at the grocery store or around town, flip through it while you're waiting on a checkout line. If it's only ten or fifteen dollars, consider buying it. Making these kinds of investments is bound to save you money over time.

Buy Annual Passes

If you have kids who enjoy frequent visits to a nearby children's museum, science center, aquarium, or zoo, look into buying annual passes. Often these passes pay for themselves in three visits and serve as a nice free source of entertainment the rest of the year. In addition, a number of reciprocity programs will allow annual passholders half-price or free access to hundreds of similar locations nationwide. This can come in handy if your family takes frequent day trips and vacations. To find out more about reciprocity programs, visit ChildrensMuseums.org, ASTC.org, and AZA.org.

Enjoy the Great Outdoors

They don't call this country "America the beautiful" for nothing. We truly live in one of the most beautiful countries in the world. Getting out and experiencing the gorgeous landscapes around you is one of the best ways to enjoy free entertainment and stay fit year round. Regardless of where you live in the country, there should be a number of beautiful locations within a reasonable driving distance from your front door. A good way to learn about nearby scenic spots is to purchase a hiking or outdoor recreational guidebook for your state. You should be able to find a used copy of such a book on Amazon.com, AbeBooks.com, or Powells.com for just a few dollars.

If you live near a national or state park you particularly like but that charges an entry fee, again, look into annual passes. The America the Beautiful Pass gives you access to all of our national parks and federal recreation sites, covering over two thousand locations nationwide. The cost for an annual pass is currently eighty dollars, however, if you are a senior citizen or have a disability, you can get a lifetime pass for next to nothing.

Pack a Snack and Bring Your Lunch

One of the easiest ways to save money during outings is to pack a snack and bring your lunch. Sandwiches and fruit make for a quick, inexpensive lunch, and granola or nutritional bars can be thrown into your bag at the last minute for a satisfying healthy snack. Doing this even occasionally can end up saving you hundreds of dollars throughout the year. In addition, you will probably enjoy food from your home more than the overpriced junk food available at most entertainment destinations.

HOW MUCH MONEY CAN YOU SAVE ON ENTERTAINMENT?

Saving method	Average savings
Buying the Entertainment Book	50% at restaurants and on local entertainment
Buying movie passes	30% at most nationwide cinemas
Buying tickets from a discounted ticket booth	40% of the tickets' face value
Buying annual passes for recreational sites	50% if you use it six times a year

CHAPTER TEN

VACATIONS AND TRAVEL EXPENSES

Only the privileged few can afford not to shop around for reasonable prices on airline tickets and other travel expenses. The rest of us do the best we can to travel without depleting our savings. Trying to put together an inexpensive trip can be a nightmare of surfing through endless websites, or it can be an enjoyable experience when it's done in the right way. I am confident that if you take the following suggestions, you will end up paying the rock-bottom rates that we all know are out there, with minimal effort.

AIRLINE TICKETS

Avoid Price Hikes

The best way to save money on airline tickets is to make your reservations far enough in advance to avoid automatic price hikes. Generally, any ticket booked at least twenty-one days before you fly is considered an advance reservation. All airlines operate differently, but usually prices increase after the twenty-first day and continue to jump up fifteen and seven days before takeoff. With a little foresight you should be able to avoid these increases and save yourself hundreds of dollars.

If your travel dates are at least a month away, you may want to track ticket prices. Owing to supply and demand, fluctuating fuel costs, and a number of other factors, the cost of airfare can jump and fall spontaneously. As opposed to monitoring prices yourself, use one of the many websites that can do this task for you. Most flight-tracking websites send out e-mail alerts when prices dip, providing an easy and stress-free way to find good bargains.

Yapta.com is a great website to use for this purpose. Yapta's search engine compiles data from over two hundred travel websites and routinely seems to find better rates than its competition. This is the same search engine that Kayak .com uses, which has earned it endorsements from *Travel and Leisure, PC World,* and *Time* magazine.

Besides tracking prices before you fly, Yapta also tracks fares after you've purchased your ticket. If the price of your ticket drops after you buy it, you may be entitled to a refund for the difference between the two rates. Every airline has different policies concerning price drops, and thankfully Yapta keeps track of all this for you. While benefiting from a price drop may sound like a shot in the dark, Yapta has already helped consumers identify over 400 million dollars in such refunds since the site launched in 2007.

Get Multiple Quotes

If you plan on flying within thirty days and don't have the luxury of tracking fares, use five or six travel websites to search for tickets. Visiting more websites than this will rarely save you money and will only cause unnecessary frustration. Kayak.com, AirGorilla.com, Priceline.com, Expedia.com, and Orbitz.com are all good choices. SkyScanner.com and Momondo.com are also good websites to visit when you are looking for international flights.

When you are comparing tickets, airfare shouldn't be the only factor you consider, especially if you are embarking on a long-haul flight. For an extra fifty dollars you can usually avoid lengthy layovers or have a much more comfortable trip. If you are unfamiliar with some of the airlines offering appealing tickets, visit AirlineQuality.com. This helpful website provides in-depth information on almost every active airline in the world.

After narrowing down your options to a handful of flights, be sure to review the baggage allowance and change and cancellation fees for each ticket you are considering. Keep in mind that travel arrangements don't always go as planned and that last-minute changes can be expensive. Having foresight into potential adjustments can end up saving you hundreds of dollars down the line.

To ensure that your change and calculation fees are as low as possible, it's a good idea to buy your tickets directly from airline carriers. Generally, your final cost will be the same or a few dollars less than the prices displayed on travel websites. Even if you find a slightly less expensive price elsewhere, the rigid policies attached to your ticket are likely to outweigh any savings offered.

Track Your Frequent Flyer Miles

Depending on how often you fly, it may or may not be worth your while to sign up for frequent flyer programs. It you fly only once or twice a year, signing up for these programs is likely to be a waste of your time. Unlike a few years ago, most frequent flyer miles now expire in a year or two and are rarely cashed in.

Conversely, if you fly several times a year, frequent flyer programs can save you money. When this is the case, use an online service to track your miles as opposed to tracking them yourself. AwardWallet.com is currently the most popular mile-tracking website available owing to its helpful features and user-friendly layout. The basic edition of AwardWallet is completely free to use and includes e-mail reminders shortly before your miles expire. Members are also able to track other award programs such as credit card and hotel points. UsingMiles.com and MileageManager.com offer similar services with slight variations.

HOTEL ROOMS

Visit TripAdvisor for Budget Recommendations

TripAdvisor.com is a great website to use to find budget hotels. The key advantage to visiting TripAdvisor instead of another travel website is having the freedom to read numerous consumer reviews for each hotel you are considering. This is particularly helpful for budget hotels because of inconsistencies in quality and comfort.

Although it's true that most travel websites now feature consumer reviews, TripAdvisor probably has more comments than all the others combined. In addition, unlike other websites, TripAdvisor has a good system in place to prevent owner-manipulated and malicious reviews. This includes reviewing IP addresses, e-mail addresses, and content before any comments are posted on the website. As a second line of defense, when visitors read reviews that are out of sync with their hotel experiences, they are encouraged to report them to TripAdvisor to be examined and potentially removed. As a result of these security measures, TripAdvisor is trusted by more than 200 million travelers each month.

Visit Priceline for Mid-Range or Luxury Hotels

Priceline.com is a good website to visit when you are looking for mid-range or luxury hotels. This innovative website provides an outlet where hotel owners can market their unfilled rooms at deep discounts, without cutting their advertised rates. They are able to do this through Priceline's "Name Your Own Price" application. When you use this bidding tool, Priceline will not reveal the name of the hotel with which you are making a reservation until after it's booked. Although this may sound like a major drawback, it really isn't. Priceline does let you choose the district in which you want to stay as well as the star rating of your hotel. Unlike budget accommodations, most hotels are comparable to those with the same rating.

When you place a bid with Priceline's "Name Your Own Price" application, it will be accepted or rejected immediately. If your bid is accepted, you are locked in to the reservation. If it's rejected, you can try again with a higher bid after twenty-four hours. To avoid overpaying for your reservation, it's a good idea to visit one of the many websites that track recently accepted bids on Priceline. BetterBidding.com and TheBiddingTraveler.com are both good websites to consult.

If your travel dates are a few weeks away, start your bidding at ten dollars less than the best rate observed on one of these websites. If your bid is rejected, increase it each day in five dollar increments. Ideally, you should start bidding around three weeks before your trip.

The biggest drawback to using Priceline's "Name Your Own Price" negotiator is that you can't change or cancel your reservation after it's booked. If this is a concern, you should explore other ways to save money on hotels. If it isn't, you are unlikely to find a better deal on any other website.

Visit Hotwire for Specific Amenities

Hotwire.com is similar to Priceline.com in many ways. Generally, hotels on Priceline are about 10 percent cheaper than hotels on Hotwire, but Hotwire will offer you a little more control over the hotel room you're booking. Unlike Priceline, Hotwire allows you to view the specific amenities that each hotel offers, such as a pool, gym, or kitchenette. If any of these things are important to you, it may be worth sacrificing a few extra dollars to know exactly what you're getting. Also, Hotwire does not operate in a bidding fashion, which makes it easier to make a reservation.

Unfortunately, like Priceline, Hotwire will not allow you to cancel or change your reservation and will not reveal the names of featured hotels until after your reservation is made. The reason for this is once again to protect hotels from getting into bidding wars by cutting advertised rates. As a result, even though better deals can usually be found on Priceline, Hotwire is consistently cheaper than other travel websites.

Visit Fee-Free Websites for Complete Flexibility

When you require the flexibility to be able to change or cancel your reservation, your best bet is visiting fee-free websites. A few of the mainstream travel websites, such as Hotels.com and Expedia.com, let you book reservations without charging you cancellation fees if your travel plans change. However, featured hotels often have their own cancellation policies, so be sure to look into this prior to making a reservation.

If you are a AAA member, you can also get discounts for many popular hotel chains around the country. Although these discounts won't match up to the savings available on Priceline or Hotwire, you should have the freedom to change your travel dates if needed.

Consider Renting a Home Instead of a Hotel

Renting a home for a few days or weeks has become a popular alternative to staying in hotels. This is ideal when you are traveling with a large family or group. Most vacation rentals are similar to hotels in the sense that their owners rarely live there. Instead, they are continuously rented out and maintained by cleaning services.

In addition to the added advantage of having a kitchen and living room, many home rentals include amenities like a pool or hot tub. Practically every home rental also comes equipped with a TV, DVD player, washing machine and dryer, and kitchenware. While renting simple homes is an option, many families who enjoy vacation rentals opt to rent luxurious million dollar homes. The cost for these rentals is typically less than two hundred dollars a day, and the locations can be stunning.

Vacation rentals are available in just about every traveled town and city in the country. It's ideal to make your reservation two to three months in advance; however, if you are in a pinch and need a rental next week, you should be able to find something.

The best place to start your hunt for vacation rentals is on VRBO.com. This is currently the most popular and widely used website for this purpose, with great security systems in place and a large number of listings. If you can't find a desirable rental on VRBO.com, visit HomeAway.com and VacationHomeRentals.com. These are good secondary sites to use that also have reputable security systems to put your mind at ease when making a deposit.

CAR RENTALS

Use Entertainment Coupons

Unlike discounts on airline tickets and hotel reservations, discounts on car rentals are not so easy to come by online. The prices quoted on mainstream travel websites are usually the same or higher than standard rates. Thankfully, there are a few other ways to save money on this expense.

As discussed in the previous chapter, the Entertainment Book can help you save money on many things. Among the coupons in each edition are those for America's biggest car rental agencies. Typically, discounts can be found for Avis, Budget, Alamo, National, Hertz, and Enterprise. Utilizing one these coupons should reduce the cost of your rental by 10 to 20 percent.

Depending on where you are going, you may be able to save even more money if you make your reservation with an independent local agency. Because these companies have lower operating costs, you can often rent vehicles from them for much lower rates than mainstream chains. CarRental-Express.com is great website to visit if you are open to this option. This website currently features hundreds of independent rental agencies throughout the United States.

Don't Overpay for Insurance

After piecing together a great deal, often what sours the mood of thrifty car renters are the overpriced insurance charges we all feel cornered into accepting. With a little luck you may be able to avoid this expense if you have free complementary coverage from one of your credit cards or if you have an auto insurance policy that covers rentals. However, if you don't have rental coverage, be sure to review what you are buying before signing away an extra thirty dollars a day. Although purchasing collision and liability coverage makes good financial sense, you should think hard before spending money on other types of insurance. Anything related to personal injuries will usually be covered under your health care plan. Other insurance add-ons rarely benefit drivers, even when accidents occur.

Explore Different Rate Plans

When you are making your reservation, do your best to avoid daily rate plans. Weekly and weekend rate plans are almost always a better option, offering up to a 50 percent discount per day. In addition, some agencies may offer other promotional rate plans that are worth exploring.

Sometimes even renting a car for a day longer than you need it will save you money by giving you access to better rates. Doing this won't be an inconvenience as you can always return your vehicle early. You can inquire about different rate plans over the phone or in person when you are making your reservation.

SideStep Extra Fees and Charges

Extra rental fees and charges tend to add up quickly and can significantly impact your final bill. Airport pickup fees tend to be the worst offender of these often outrageous charges. In addition to charging extra fees and taxes, rental agencies near the airport often have a completely different pricing structure than other branches. If it's not a hassle to rent a car near your hotel, see what a taxi will cost you to get to where you are staying, and compare this cost to the amount of money you will save by not renting a car at the airport. Depending on your destination, inner-city rentals can cost as much as fifty dollars less per day.

Gas refill fees are another common way for rental agencies to hike up your final bill. If your car had a full tank of gas when you received it, make sure to return it in the same fashion. You should also avoid prepaid gas options. Rarely will you use the exact amount of gas to make these packages worthwhile.

CRUISES

Plan Ahead

Cruises tend to be the best-valued vacations dollar for dollar, but they are not for everybody. Generally, they are less adventurous and more restrictive than land travel. However, the flip side to this is that they tend to be more relaxing and indulgent. Most cruise lines offer resort amenities at far more affordable rates than land vacations. In addition, unlike at a resort, when you take a cruise, you also get the added advantage of being able to visit multiple destinations in your region of choice.

Cruise prices do not fluctuate as widely as airplane ticket

prices, but usually you can get a better deal if you book your cabin at the right time. If you are planning to take a cruise during the summer or during a holiday week, you would be well advised to make your booking at least six months in advance. When you are traveling during a shoulder season, such as April to mid-June, making your reservation two to three months in advance should be a safe bet and may yield good discounts as a result of unsold cabins on larger ships.

For ultra spontaneous travelers, it's also possible to get great deals at the last minute. Often cruise lines will attempt to get whatever they can for unsold cabins days before their ships set sail. This can be a good excuse to treat yourself to a nice vacation if you have the freedom to travel at the drop of a dime. For the rest of us, planning ahead is the best way to save money at sea.

Research Cruise Lines

Most travelers have an idea of where they would like to visit before planning their vacation. That being said, unlike for land travel, when you go on a cruise, the ship on which you are traveling is just as important as the destination. All major cruise lines seem to have their own lifestyle niche. Some cater to spa and gourmet travelers, whereas others focus on nightlife, entertainment, or romantic offerings. CruiseCritic .com is a great website to visit to find cruise lines that best suit your needs. This useful site provides expert and consumer reviews for just about everything related to cruising and can be an invaluable asset when planning a trip. In addition to researching cruise lines, CruiseCritic can also help you choose itineraries, shore excursions, travel seasons, and even individual ships within a fleet. Spending adequate time on the site is bound to enrich your holiday, even if you are an avid cruiser.

Get Multiple Quotes

After narrowing your trip down to a few options, take a handful of minutes to collect quotes directly from each cruise line you are considering. You can do this by visiting their websites or giving them a call. Then, pay a visit to CruiseCompete.com, a site that allows you to request specific cruise quotes from an ever-growing pool of travel agents who compete to offer you the best rates for each of your submissions. Travel agents can often come up with the best rates for cruises owing to group buying deals. Even when they aren't in a position to offer you group rates, travel agents are likely to explore other ways to save you money, which may include giving you a few hundred dollars in onboard ship credit. Because it makes little difference with whom you book your cruise, you should always take the best offer you can find.

CruiseCompete does not pass your contact information on to travel agents. Instead, they will send you e-mails when different agents offer competitive quotes. When you submit requests on the site, be sure to include the best quotes you have already received in the comment box at the foot of the online submission form. Taking a moment to do this will ensure that you only receive offers that are worth reviewing.

Book Shore Excursions Independently

Shore excursions are tours in or around the places that you will visit during your cruise. Depending on where your cruise is going, you may not want to bother with shore excursions altogether. Generally, in cities, you can do just fine taking taxis and buses to the many places you want to see. This option should be substantially cheaper than booking tours, while allowing you greater freedom to explore what you want for however long you like. Buying a guidebook for the region to which you are traveling can help you piece together independent explorations without headaches and worries.

When it comes to wildlife-viewing tours or other adventurous outings where guides are necessary, it's a good idea to book shore excursions ahead of time. Typically, the tours available through your cruise line will be a poor value compared to similar tours offered by independent companies. The best source for information on shore excursions is CrusieCritic.com. On the message boards of CruiseCritic you will find numerous recommendations from fellow cruisers that will help guide you to a number of reasonable options.

ADDITIONAL TRAVEL SUGGESTIONS

Invest in a Guidebook

Regardless of where you are visiting, a guidebook can save you money and enrich your vacation. Among the many popular guidebooks, the Lonely Planet series stands alone. Since its humble beginnings more than forty years ago, Lonely Planet has been using a highly successful formula to steer travelers in the right direction.

Like most travel guidebooks, Lonely Planet provides in-depth information on pretravel preparation, local attractions, hotels, restaurants, nightlife, regional history, and culture. However, what truly makes this series stand out are its detailed descriptions of how to see, do, and buy all things you want for a fair market rate. Whether you are traveling on a shoestring or have endless amounts of money, each guidebook is bound to reduce your expenses.

If you have reservations about spending twenty dollars for the latest edition of a guidebook you require, you can always purchase a slightly outdated edition for a few dollars on Amazon.com. Naturally, its information won't be as up to date, but it should still save you money.

If you are just taking a daytrip or going somewhere for a weekend, visit TripAdvisor.com for helpful advice. TripAdvisor provides free information on attractions, sightseeing, and entertainment for travel destinations all over the world.

Don't Overspend on Souvenirs

Most of us like to get a silly T-shirt or a souvenir when we are traveling. I would not suggest trying to avoid this expense altogether, but it's a good idea to set a clear budget with family members for shopping on the road. This is especially helpful when you are traveling with kids. A successful strategy that a number of families have implemented is giving each member of the family a set souvenir budget. This budget can vary depending on your financial situation, but twenty dollars per person should be more than sufficient. Utilizing this practice can also be a good way to give kids a money lesson and make them think twice before spending their money on junky impulse purchases.

Save Money on Meals

When it comes to dining on the road, a good way to save money is to prepare your own meals from time to time in your hotel. Buying sandwich makings at a local grocery store is an easy, inexpensive meal option. Preparing your own sandwiches should cost you only a couple of dollars per meal and can be done in just a few minutes. If your hotel room has a refrigerator, microwave, or kitchenette, you will have endless options for in-room food preparation.

Restaurant.com can also help you save money during getaways. Because you can search for restaurants by zip code on the site, you will often find dining certificates for locations right down the road from your hotel. When you are traveling, there's no reason why you can't save money and still enjoy all the things you want to do. Hopefully, the suggestions in this chapter will help you find the balance between these two common goals.

HOW MUCH MONEY CAN YOU SAVE ON VACATION AND TRAVEL EXPENSES?

Saving method	Average savings
Buying airline tickets 21 days in advance	25% on airfare
Booking hotels through Priceline.com	30% on mid-range and luxury hotel rooms
Using Entertainment Book coupons for car rentals	15% less than advertised rates
Booking cruises through CruiseCompete.com	10% less than advertised rates

CHAPTER ELEVEN

CREDIT CARDS AND BANKING

Like most Americans, you probably have a few credit cards that give you a small amount of cash back or rewards points every time you use them. While something is better than nothing, the odds are pretty good that you can double this figure by taking a few minutes to compare the best credit cards for which you can qualify. Similarly, you don't have to settle for bank accounts with miniscule interest rates any longer. You can now open checking accounts with small financial institutions that offer the same security and protection as national banks, while yielding about twenty times more interest. The following tips will guide you through this process and help you earn effortless money with credit cards and accounts that are compatible with your lifestyle.

CREDIT CARDS

Review Your Credit Reports and FICO Scores

Cash-back and rewards credit cards offer a unique opportunity to make money every time you buy something. As long as you pay off your balance each month, this is free money that goes right into your pocket. Regardless of what you may have read elsewhere, there's no such thing as a "best" credit card. Different cards are tailored to different lifestyles and spending habits. As a result, it's a good idea to compare credit cards every so often.

Ideally, before you begin comparing credit cards, you should review your credit reports and FICO scores if it has been more than a year since you last did so. Doing this will ensure that inaccurate information is not affecting your credit and will give you an idea which cards you are likely to qualify for. The best place to get a copy of your credit reports is at AnnualCreditReport.com, the only federally sanctioned website offering free credit reports from three reporting credit bureaus. When you review your credit history, don't be surprised if you find inaccurate information. According to a recent government study, as many as 40 million Americans have errors on their credit reports. Around half of these errors are serious enough to lower credit scores. If you see something that you believe is inaccurate, file a dispute with the credit bureau that provided the report.

Unfortunately, these free reports do not include your FICO scores. For the purpose of applying for new credit cards, you can get an idea of your average FICO score free of charge at CreditKarma.com. Unlike most free FICO score websites, CreditKarma does not have any hidden fees or obligations. In addition, it should take all of two minutes to preview your score, and you are welcome to track it throughout the year.

The only downside to using this free service is that the score you will be viewing is not one of your actual FICO scores. However, CreditKarma does show you your Transrisk score, which is produced by TransUnion. TransUnion is one of the three reporting credit bureaus that actually helped develop the FICO scoring module. Most consumers find that this score is fairly close to their average FICO score, making it a good free option for credit card hunting. Similarly to using AnnualCreditReport, using CreditKarma will not adversely affect your FICO scores, as monitoring your personal credit history is considered a soft inquiry.

If you want to see your actual FICO scores, either visit MyFICO.com or get them directly from the three major credit bureaus at Transunion.com, Experian.com, and Equifax.com. You will have to pay a small fee or sign up for some kind of credit monitoring service through all four websites, but at least you know that you are dealing with trustworthy sources.

Match Credit Cards with Your Spending Habits

Visiting websites that compare credit cards is the easiest way to find plastic that is tailored to your needs. The best websites to consult are the ones that don't use search engine software and make personal recommendations. CreditKarma.com and WiseBread.com are good options that take the time to do this.

If you plan to use your credit cards for saving purposes, don't let interest rates influence your evaluation. As long as you are committed to paying off your balance each month, you will never have to pay interest, making it an irrelevant topic.

Credit card policies and perks are constantly changing, and numerous new cash-back and rewards cards seem to pop up each year. Having said that, for the past few years the Blue Cash Preferred card, the Citi Double Cash card, and the PenFed Travel Rewards card have all been top choices to consider. Using one of these cards, or a combination of them, should save you four hundred to one thousand dollars per year.

If your credit isn't good enough to qualify for a premium card, get the best plastic you can. With a little determination, you should be able to get a lucrative credit card in a year or two. You can find many good books and free information online to help you improve your FICO scores. Dedicating time and effort to this cause is bound to pay off in the long run.

Increase Your Earnings

Acquiring multiple credit cards that offer different types of benefits is an easy way to increase your cash back and/or reward points. For example, if you have good credit, you should be able to get a card that pays you upward of 5 percent cash back on groceries, gas, or airfare. If you spend significant money on all of these things, it makes sense to get all of them. In addition, credit cards like the US Bank Cash+ card, the Chase Freedom card, and the Discover It card all offer 5 percent cash back in several rotating categories. As long as you keep track of these categories, you will be able to save extra money by using them for a number of purchases throughout the year. Similarly, getting credit cards with appealing signup bonuses can be another way to make money with minimal effort. Just be careful not to apply for too many cards at one time, as doing so can negatively impact your credit scores.

Finally, if you are ever accidentally late with a payment and receive a late payment fee, call your card issuer and ask to have it removed. Most issuers will be happy to do this for you, at least the first couple of times it occurs.

BANK ACCOUNTS

Open a Rewards Checking Account

In the past, a certificate of deposit (CD) has always been viewed as the best way to earn high-interest rates on your savings. The downside to putting your money in a CD is that you cannot access it for a set amount of time, unless you are willing to break your contract and pay early withdrawal fees. As a result, CDs appeal mainly to high-income earners.

Thanks to the recent online banking boom, the entire game has changed. You can now open a high-yield checking account that outperforms even five-year CDs. Because these accounts allow you to access your money any time you need to, they are great choices for everyday banking. Typically, high-yield checking accounts are offered by community banks and credit unions. Like checking accounts at national banks, most of these accounts are FDIC insured, or in the case of credit unions, NCUA insured. FDIC and NCUA accounts are fully insured by federal agencies, as long as your account balance does not exceed $250,000.

Rewards checking accounts currently offer higher interest rates than other options. At the time of publication, many of these accounts offered a 3 percent annual percentage yield (APY) on account balances up to fifteen thousand dollars and a 1 percent APY on the portion of balances beyond this figure. Generally, rewards checking accounts don't have balance requirements or monthly service fees. However, they typically require a monthly direct deposit and ten monthly debit card transactions. You aren't penalized for failing to meet these requirements, but you won't earn interest during any month that you don't meet them.

Banks and credit unions offering rewards checking

usually have a limited number of branches. To make these accounts appeal to consumers across the country, they typically reimburse account holders up to twenty dollars in ATM fees every month. In most cases, earned interest and ATM reimbursements are disbursed on a monthly basis.

The most intimidating aspect of rewards checking accounts is their debit card transaction requirements. These requirements can be particularly challenging if you are going out of your way to use cash-back and/or rewards credit cards. You can overcome this obstacle by restricting the use of your debit card to inexpensive purchases. This strategy works best if you make two or three small purchases each week. If you don't, you are probably better off putting your money in a standard high-yield checking account. These accounts have very few requirements yet still have an APY of up to 1 percent. While earning 1 percent interest may not sound too appealing, keep in mind that this is about ten times higher than the average interest rates for checking accounts at national banks.

Visit Bank Account Comparison Websites

The easiest way to find high-yield bank accounts is to visit websites that compare current interest rates. For rewards checking accounts, use DepositAccounts.com. If you are looking for a standard high-yield checking account with few or no requirements, visit MyBankTracker.com or BankRate.com.

Before you select an account, you should review a couple things. First and foremost, make sure that the account is FDIC or NCUA insured. Then, check how long it has had its current interest rate in place. Financial institutions with a past history of interest rate consistency are more likely to maintain their current rates. There's nothing worse than opening a high-yield bank account, only to find out weeks later that its interest rate has been lowered. Reviewing this information should greatly reduce the odds of that outcome.

Maximize Your Savings

If you open a rewards checking account, make sure you routinely meet its monthly requirements. If these requirements prove to be too challenging, don't hesitate to switch to a more suitable account. Keeping your money in a high-yield account only makes sense if you are earning interest on a regular basis.

When you need to buy checkbooks, you are usually better off purchasing them online than through your bank or credit union. For good-quality, inexpensive checks, visit WalMart-Checks.com or CostcoChecks.com (if you have a Costco membership). Both sites sell checks for approximately half the amount that banks charge and have a good assortment of personal and business backgrounds. If you want a wider range of choices, visit ChecksUnlimited.com.

Regardless of the high-yield account you select, it's still a good idea to have a bank account in your area of residence. A local account allows you the freedom to cash personal checks without having to mail them to your bank or credit union. Also, if you occasionally get offers in the mail from different banks giving away one hundred dollars to open a checking account, look into it. You can usually close these accounts after three months without any penalties or fees. Some of these accounts require a monthly direct deposit of a hundred dollars or so, but others do not. If a direct deposit is required, you should be able to have a small portion of your paycheck put into this account, while still having the majority of your money go into your primary bank account. (Unfortunately, this can't be done with Social Security checks.) In fact, you can typically take advantage of these offers over and over again with the same banks, as long as it has been over a year since you closed your last account with them. My wife and I have personally made well over one thousand dollars by capitalizing on such offers.

PAYING BILLS

Set Up Automatic Bill Payments

Americans spend an average of twenty-two hours per year paying bills. Despite this hefty investment of time, many of us are late with a payment now and then. The easiest way to reduce time spent dealing with bills and to safeguard yourself from late payment fees is to set up automatic bill payments with a credit card or a checking account.

You should be able to set up automatic payments with a number of your current service providers. This arrangement can usually be made on the merchant's website or over the phone. Just be sure to double-check that you won't be charged a fee for this convenience.

Review Your Bills

Despite making payments automatically, you don't want to switch to autopilot mode with your bills. It's imperative that you continue to review your monthly bills as they come in the mailbox or arrive in e-statements. Telecom providers are particularly notorious for making billing mistakes. Carefully reviewing every bill is the only way to catch overcharges and have them refunded back to your credit card or bank account. When you catch billing errors, let your provider know that in addition to being issued a refund, you expect to be compensated for the amount of time wasted dealing with their inability to bill you correctly. By simply suggesting this, you are likely to be reimbursed for your time and frustration.

Monitor Your Transactions

Monitoring your credit card and bank transactions is also essential to good money management. At the very least, make sure you review your monthly statements for these accounts.

If you see a charge to a merchant that you don't recall making, call your credit card issuer or bank and ask for more details.

In addition to reviewing statements, many consumers find it helpful to use a personal finance application. Some of the better personal finance applications allow you to view all your credit cards, bank accounts, and investment accounts in one place. Mint.com is a great website that offers this service free of cost. In addition to displaying all of your financial accounts together, Mint automatically categorizes all your transitions. This allows you to track your expenses, if you so desire. Thanks to Mint's bank-level security and e-mail alerts, you need not worry about compromising the protection of this information.

If you are interested in creating and sticking to a budget, you are probably better off using a different application. You Need A Budget (YNAB) personal finance software has been a long-standing consumer favorite and consistently receives better reviews than other options. This, or a similar application, should cost you around sixty dollars.

HOW MUCH MONEY CAN YOU SAVE WITH CREDIT CARDS AND BANK ACCOUNTS?

Saving method	Average savings
Using premium cash-back credit cards	5% in many shopping categories
Using a rewards checking account	3% interest on your account balance
Getting overdraft and late payment fees waived	100% of accidental fees
Buying checkbooks online	50% on basic checkbooks

START SAVING TODAY

Now that you have read this book, it's important to put a game plan in place to start saving money. One of the easiest ways to get started is to create a list of saving methods that can be implemented immediately and are compatible with your lifestyle. This list should include many of the suggestions that target your monthly bills and expenses.

Once you have made this list, give yourself a realistic timeline to complete it. Then, over the next few days or weeks, slowly chip away at tasks whenever you find time. Keep in mind that you are essentially throwing away money by not completing certain steps in a timely manner. Maintaining this mind-set should help you finish your list by your self-imposed deadline.

Besides the saving methods that impact your monthly expenses, you should find many other suggestions that can save you money throughout the year as different circumstances arise. Keep this book in a place where you can quickly access it, so it can be used as a reference guide at these times.

Staying committed to these saving methods is crucial to reaping the rewards they offer. After all, knowing how to save money is only half the battle. The other half is having the motivation and discipline to make it happen.

ACKNOWLEDGMENTS

The creation of this book would not have been possible without the help and support of many people. First, I would like to express deep appreciation to my wife Urja, who supported me throughout this process; my parents Sharon and David and my Aunt Hope and Uncle Mike, who instilled many frugal values in me at an early age; and my brother and best friend, Josh, who provided numerous helpful suggestions.

I would also like to thank Melanie Austin for her insightful editing. Far more than an editor, she was a partner on this book. Holly T. Monteith for her detailed copyediting and creative suggestions, CJ McDaniel for creating a beautiful cover, Rosamond Grupp for putting together a magnificent interior design, and Julia Thomas, Sherry Heinitz, Leslie Carman and Ben Hanawalt for their invaluable contributions.

All my readers, past, present, and future. May you save money effortlessly for many years to come.

ABOUT THE AUTHOR

Richard Syrop grew up in a family that viewed saving money as a passion, hobby, and lifestyle. Over the years, he has personally tested just about every saving method imaginable. Dissatisfied with conventional ways to reduce expenditures, Richard developed a unique approach to savings that does not require personal sacrifice. He has taught these saving methods in seminars throughout the country. Richard's love for writing and frugality led to the creation of this book. He lives in Seattle, Washington, with his wife, Urja.

INDEX

CPSIA information can be obtained at www.ICGtesting.com
Printed in the USA
BVOW06s1816040815

411797BV00008B/42/P

9 780989 015608